MW00388552

Real Italian Food
for People
with Diabetes

REAL ITALIAN FOOD FOR PEOPLE WITH DIABETES

Doris Cross

PRIMA HEALTH
A DIVISION OF PRIMA PUBLISHING

© 1999 by Doris Cross

All rights reserved. No part of this book may be reproduced or transmitted in any form or by any means, electronic or mechanical, including photocopying, recording, or by any information storage or retrieval system, without written permission from Prima Publishing, except for the inclusion of quotations in a review.

Warning—Disclaimer

This book is not intended to provide medical advice and is sold with the understanding that the publisher and the author are not liable for the misconception or misuse of information provided. The author and Prima Publishing shall have neither liability nor responsibility to any person or entity with respect to any loss, damage, or injury caused or alleged to be caused directly or indirectly by the information contained in this book or the use of any products mentioned. Readers should not use any of the products discussed in this book without the advice of a medical professional.

Nutritional Analyses

A per serving nutritional breakdown is provided for each recipe. If a range is given for an ingredient amount, the breakdown is based on the smaller number. If a range is given for servings, the breakdown is based on the larger number. If a choice of ingredients is given in an ingredient listing, the breakdown is calculated using the first choice. Nutritional content may vary depending on the specific brands or types of ingredients used. "Optional" ingredients or those for which no specific amount is stated are not included in the breakdown.

On the cover: *Lasagna (page 140), Garlic Toast with Cheese and Tomato (page 240), and Zesty Salad with Parmesan (page 73).*

PRIMA HEALTH and colophon are trademarks of Prima Communications, Inc.

Interior illustrations by Mary Rich

Library of Congress Cataloging-in-Publication Data on file

ISBN 0-7615-1493-7

99 00 01 02 03 II 10 9 8 7 6 5 4 3 2 1

Printed in the United States of America

HOW TO ORDER

Single copies may be ordered from Prima Publishing, P.O. Box 1260BK, Rocklin, CA 95677; telephone (916) 632-4400. Quantity discounts are also available. On your letterhead, include information concerning the intended use of the books and the number of books you wish to purchase.

Visit us online at www.primahealth.com

To the best of the best. This book is respectfully
dedicated to Larry W. Burns, Ph.D., Senator
Mike Morgan, and Kathleen Harder, M.D.

CONTENTS

ACKNOWLEDGMENTS

This book would not have been possible without the help of some very caring people: Dr. Larry Burns, Senator Mike Morgan, and Dr. Kathleen Harder. Thanks would never be enough for what they have done for me. These are three of the very best people in their fields and deserve a tremendous amount of credit for their kindness and caring and for the quality of work they perform.

Another special person who helped me tremendously was Adran Wagner. She is a wonderful caring lady and I appreciate her very much.

My good friend Alice Williams deserves tremendous credit for helping me in the kitchen, cooking and tasting. Her humor and laughter have always kept me going. Some of her own creations are in this book. Try them; she is such a wonderful cook.

Hugh Merrill and his wife, Kathy, are always there for anything I need, especially my computer problems. They are friends who I can always count on. They are two very special people. Hugh prepares all of my manuscripts on the computer, to go to my publisher. I don't know what I would do without him.

Rhonda Merrill has been excellent at proofing manuscripts and helping me out. I appreciate her hard work.

Always a thanks goes to an old friend, Ron Wittwer, for being supportive in my work and who made it financially possible for me to begin writing my very first book several years ago.

Jamie Miller, my acquisitions editor at Prima Publishing, is the best. Also, Michelle McCormack, my project editor, who makes my part of the job so easy because she is so efficient.

A very special thank you goes to Maurice Gershon, who always supports me in any of my ventures. She is the dearest friend.

A special thank you to Janelle Walker for her friendship, understanding, and support.

Stacy Sawyer has been my right hand with proofing and corrections and I appreciate so much all the hard and careful work she has done on this book. I always know I can depend on her.

Abby and Hannah Stokes and Sharon Brown have absolutely been my best tasters and critics. I enjoyed so much having them try the recipes.

Another official taster, K.J. Aranda, is so fun and so sweet. She is always willing to taste anything and give me an honest opinion.

Of course, my good friends in New Jersey, Erma and Elmo Brown, always do their part for me as far as book promotions on the east coast. Keep up the good work, guys.

Rick and Rodette Green are such good friends and have been very supportive of my cookbook writing for many years now. Thank you both, for your friendship and interest.

Thanks to the girls at Dr. Kathleen Harder's office, Diana Spiva and Jeannie Drew. These two always have smiles on their faces. Their tasting expertise leans more towards other types of foods, which I am not at liberty to mention, but I can always count on them for anything I need.

Thank you to all of my family members and friends who support whatever I am working on at the present time. I am so grateful to have this quality of people around me.

INTRODUCTION

Every year, thousands of people discover they have diabetes. It can be a very scary disease. One of the most important aspects of dealing with diabetes is food intake.

Contrary to common assumption, diabetic food and cooking does not have to be boring or tasteless. Take pasta. To many of us, it's more satisfying than a lot of other foods. It's more substantial and filling—or at least, seems to be. (Perhaps it's all that heavenly cheese and starch.) And for most of us, our first favorite foods were macaroni or spaghetti. There's just something special about Italian food. The aroma of simmering spaghetti sauce on the stove, or yummy pizza or lasagna baking in the oven seems to warm us inside.

Also, there are so many wonderful vegetables that are "good" for us in all kinds of Italian foods—especially the tomato-based dishes: onions, mushrooms, spinach, carrots, broccoli, etc. What a great way to add color and taste to any meal! Plus, many pasta and sauce dishes are easy and fast to make, and that is important to all of us. So, what's your favorite Italian food? Pizza? Lasagna? Fettuccine Alfredo? Now you can make it low fat with lighter cheeses and still remain on the diabetic eating program. The recipes in this book are healthy and delicious!

The diabetic eating program continues to evolve as new research becomes available about this disease. However, for now, the need to maintain certain lifestyle habits seems to remain fairly consistent: maintain a desirable weight, eat plenty of fiber, eat a variety of foods, try not to overeat, eat low fat, avoid most sugar, do not overeat starches, and be careful about too much sodium. Also, avoid alcohol or limit your intake. Exercise every day if at all possible and strictly follow your doctor's advice about your disease.

Check with your physician about working with a local dietitian, contact state and national chapters of the American Diabetes Association for information, look at the bookstore for books on diabetes, and, above all, take an active part in your own well-being. *So much depends on you!*

I remember when I was first diagnosed, I did everything perfectly, the medicine, the food, exercise, and so on. As my commitment began to dwindle, I lost my focus and decided, for a while, that I probably didn't even have diabetes. Big mistake. This form of denial can cost you greatly, in terms of your own health.

Diabetes can require drastic lifestyle changes that are hard for anyone to make. Try, as much as you can, to relax with your new lifestyle and after awhile it will become easier. If you ignore your diabetes, it *will not* go away. At some point, you will need to make peace with it, so you can begin to live your life feeling better again.

P.S. I've found an absolutely wonderful product called Buttermist. It's a cooking spray that has the same number of calories and same amount of fat as other nonstick cooking sprays, but the taste makes it just like spraying butter out of a can. Use it like any other nonstick cooking spray. It makes heavenly garlic toast and is wonderful on popcorn. To order Buttermist, call (888) 743-0989.

In Loving Memory of My Mom,
Verna Duckwall Walton
1910–1999

1

Dips, Sauces, and Spreads

Garlic and Olive Cream Cheese Dip

1   tub (8 ounces) fat-free cream cheese
¼   cup fat-free sour cream
2   cloves garlic, pressed
¼   cup green salad olives, drained
2   teaspoons dry onion flakes
    Black pepper to taste
    Dash of seasoned salt

Using a medium bowl, combine cream cheese and sour cream with electric mixer. Mix until smooth. Add all remaining ingredients and mix thoroughly. Chill for at least 1 hour. This is a good dip for veggies or lowfat crackers.

Each serving provides:

50	Calories	.65 g	Fat
6.58 g	Protein	311 g	Sodium
4.15 g	Carbohydrate	3.02 mg	Cholesterol

Diabetic exchanges: Lean meat, 1

Seafood Dip

10 medium shrimp, cleaned, peeled, and cooked
1 teaspoon dry onion flakes
2 teaspoons green bell pepper, finely chopped
1 clove garlic, pressed
1½ tablespoons fresh lemon juice
1 tub (8 ounces) fat-free cream cheese
2 tablespoons shredded Parmesan cheese
¼ teaspoon seasoned salt
Dash of black pepper

Chop shrimp in food processor. Add remaining ingredients and process until blended. Remove from food processor and pour into bowl. Chill for about 1 hour. Serve with lowfat crackers if desired.

Each serving provides:			
64	Calories	.70 g	Fat
10.45 g	Protein	273 g	Sodium
3.14 g	Carbohydrate	41.24 mg	Cholesterol

Diabetic exchanges: Lean meat, 1½

Cream Cheese with Sun-Dried Tomato Dip

1 tub (8 ounces) fat-free cream cheese
2 green onions, thinly sliced
2 pieces of sun-dried tomato (I use the kind in a jar packed in olive oil and rinse most of the oil off with hot water.)
½ cup fat-free sour cream
⅛ teaspoon seasoned salt
1 clove garlic, pressed

Place cream cheese in medium bowl and mix with an electric mixer until smooth. Add all remaining ingredients and mix thoroughly. Chill for at least 30 minutes before serving. Serve with crunchy, thinly sliced garlic toasts, if desired. Lowfat crackers also work well.

Each serving provides:

51	Calories	.14 g	Fat
7.2 g	Protein	208 g	Sodium
4.9 g	Carbohydrate	3.0 mg	Cholesterol

Diabetic exchanges: Very lean meat, 1

Layered Italian Pasta Dip

SERVES 12

1 cup fat-free sour cream
2 cloves garlic, pressed
⅛ teaspoon seasoned salt
1 medium onion, chopped
1 cup chopped canned tomatoes, drained
  Dash of oregano flakes
  Black pepper to taste
2 cups cooked elbow macaroni
6 strips roasted bell pepper, cut in thirds
1 cup shredded fat-free mozzarella cheese
2 teaspoons olive juice from jar of salad olives
⅓ cup green salad olives, drained
¼ cup shredded Parmesan cheese

Preheat oven to 350 degrees.

In small bowl, combine sour cream, garlic, and seasoned salt. Mix until smooth and set aside.

Spray small skillet with nonstick cooking spray. Sauté and cook chopped onion until lightly brown. Set aside to cool.

In another small bowl, combine tomatoes, oregano, and black pepper. Set aside.

Spray 9-inch square glass baking dish with nonstick cooking spray. Pour 1 cup cooked macaroni on the bottom. Spoon on the tomato mixture for next layer. Then add chopped onions. Next, pour or spoon on sour cream mixture. Then add the other cup of cooked macaroni.

Next, add roasted bell pepper strips. In small bowl, toss together mozzarella cheese and juice from olives. Top with salad olives and sprinkle on shredded Parmesan cheese.

Bake for 25 to 30 minutes. Great served with garlic toast or lowfat crackers.

Each serving provides:

82	Calories	1.17 g	Fat
6.58 g	Protein	244 g	Sodium
11.32 g	Carbohydrate	3.0 mg	Cholesterol

Diabetic exchanges: Very lean meat, 1; starch, ½

Note: This recipe is especially for all the "queens." You know who you are—enjoy!

Garlic Dip

½ fresh cucumber, peeled
1 tub (8 ounces) fat-free cream cheese
1 clove garlic, pressed
¼ teaspoon seasoned salt
1 teaspoon dry onion flakes
¼ teaspoon red pepper flakes

Lightly chop cucumber in food processor, but do not liquefy. Remove to paper towel to drain. Place all other ingredients in food processor and process until smooth. Remove to a bowl and stir in chopped cucumber. Chill for about 1 hour and serve.

Each serving provides:

30	Calories	.02 g	Fat
4.44 g	Protein	151 g	Sodium
2.58 g	Carbohydrate	2.27 mg	Cholesterol

Diabetic exchanges: Very lean meat, 1

Alice's Butter Sauce for Pasta or Veggies

SERVES 8

2 packets (½ ounce each) Butter Buds
1 tablespoon Molly McButter butter sprinkles
½ cup hot water
2 to 3 teaspoons lemon juice

Mix all ingredients with spoon in small bowl and stir until butter sprinkles and Butter Buds are dissolved.

Pour over cooked pasta or steamed veggies and serve.

Each serving provides:

11	Calories	.12 g	Fat
.04 g	Protein	199 g	Sodium
3.03 g	Carbohydrate	.03 mg	Cholesterol

Diabetic exchanges: free food

Spinach and Pine Nut Sauce for Pasta

1 tablespoon pine nuts, chopped
3 tablespoons fat-free chicken broth
1 medium onion, chopped
1 clove garlic, pressed
¾ cup fat-free chicken broth
2 cups fresh spinach, chopped fairly fine
¾ cup skim milk
  Salt and black pepper to taste
½ cup fat-free sour cream
¼ cup shredded Parmesan cheese, for garnish
3 cups cooked angel hair pasta

Spray medium saucepan with nonstick cooking spray. Add pine nuts. Stir and brown over medium-low heat. Pour the browned nuts out on a paper towel. Add 3 tablespoons chicken broth to pan. Sauté onion and garlic in broth until tender, 4 to 5 minutes. Add ¾ cup chicken broth and chopped spinach and cook over medium-low heat for 3 to 4 minutes. Stir in skim milk and continue cooking over low heat for 2 to 3 minutes. Add salt and black pepper to taste and add the toasted pine nuts. Whisk in sour cream, just before serving. Garnish with shredded Parmesan cheese and serve over angel hair pasta.

Each serving provides:			
246	Calories	3.73 g	Fat
13.05 g	Protein	489 g	Sodium
40.49 g	Carbohydrate	4.75 mg	Cholesterol

Diabetic exchanges: Lean meat, 1; starch, 1¾; vegetable, 1; fat, ½

Shrimp and Scallops in White Sauce

SERVES 4

½ small onion, chopped
1½ cups fat-free chicken broth
2 cloves garlic, pressed
½ teaspoon Molly McButter butter sprinkles
8 medium cooked shrimp
8 medium to small cooked scallops
½ cup skim milk
Salt and black pepper to taste
½ cup fat-free sour cream
3 cups cooked pasta (of your choice)

Spray skillet with nonstick cooking spray. Add onion and stir over low-medium heat until onion starts to turn clear, about 4 to 5 minutes. Add chicken broth, garlic, Molly McButter, shrimp, and scallops. Simmer over low heat for about 4 minutes. Add skim milk, salt and black pepper, and stir over medium-low heat for about 1 minute. Whisk in sour cream and simmer another minute. Serve over your favorite pasta.

Each serving provides:

239	Calories	1.23 g	Fat
17.77 g	Protein	519 g	Sodium
37.97 g	Carbohydrate	52.31 mg	Cholesterol

Diabetic exchanges: Very lean meat, 2; starch, 1¾

Red Clam Sauce for Pasta

1 can (8 ounces) tomato sauce
1 can (10 ounces) baby clams, drained and rinsed
⅓ cup clam juice
1 clove garlic, pressed
1 medium onion, chopped
¾ cup fat-free chicken broth
¼ teaspoon onion powder
⅛ teaspoon Italian seasoning
  Salt and black pepper to taste
2½ cups cooked pasta

Combine all ingredients for sauce in a medium saucepan. Simmer over low heat for 15 to 20 minutes or until onion is tender. Serve over cooked pasta.

Each serving provides:

274	Calories	1.91 g	Fat
19.56 g	Protein	605 g	Sodium
44.09 g	Carbohydrate	32.37 mg	Cholesterol

Diabetic exchanges: Lean meat, 2; starch, 2

Quick and Easy Spaghetti Sauce

½ pound ground turkey breast
1 small onion, chopped
½ cup tomato sauce
¾ cup water
½ cup fresh sliced mushrooms
2 teaspoons packaged dry spaghetti sauce mix
¼ teaspoon garlic powder
   Salt and black pepper to taste
3 cups cooked spaghetti

Spray medium skillet with nonstick cooking spray. Add ground turkey and onion and brown. Add all remaining sauce ingredients and simmer about 10 minutes. Serve over spaghetti.

Each serving provides:

238	Calories	1.72 g	Fat
19.22 g	Protein	214 g	Sodium
34.96 g	Carbohydrate	34.02 mg	Cholesterol

Diabetic exchanges: Very lean meat, 2; starch, 2

Lemon Garlic Sauce for Pasta

½ cup fat-free cream cheese
1½ tablespoons lemon juice
½ cup fat-free chicken broth
2 cloves garlic, pressed
½ teaspoon Molly McButter butter sprinkles
⅛ teaspoon black pepper
1½ cups cooked pasta

In small bowl, mix cream cheese with electric mixer until smooth. Slowly stir in lemon juice with a spoon. After lemon juice is mixed in smooth, gradually add chicken broth and stir.

Stir in all remaining ingredients, except pasta. Pour sauce mixture in small saucepan and stir over medium heat until mixture comes to a boil. Reduce heat and continue to stir for 3 to 4 minutes. Serve over cooked pasta.

Each serving provides:

220	Calories	.72 g	Fat
15.78 g	Protein	615 g	Sodium
36.61 g	Carbohydrate	5.28 mg	Cholesterol

Diabetic exchanges: Very lean meat, 2; starch, 1¾

Garlic Lovers' Pasta Sauce

SERVES 4

15 cloves peeled garlic, cut in half
 1 can (8 ounces) tomato sauce
 2 cans (14½ ounces each) diced tomatoes
¼ teaspoon Italian seasoning
 1 tablespoon dry onion flakes
½ cup fat-free chicken broth
 4 tablespoons grated Parmesan cheese, for garnish

Combine all ingredients, except Parmesan, in saucepan and simmer over low heat for 20 to 30 minutes, or until garlic is tender.

Serve over any pasta and garnish with shredded Parmesan cheese.

Each serving provides:

103	Calories	2.19	g	Fat
5.90 g	Protein	1151	g	Sodium
18.40 g	Carbohydrate	4.0	mg	Cholesterol

Diabetic exchanges: Lean meat, 1; vegetable, 2

Italian Sausage and Mushroom Sauce for Pasta

SERVES 4

- 1 link sweet Italian turkey sausage, sliced
- 1 can (10½ ounces) Campbell's 98 percent fat-free cream of mushroom soup
- ½ cup fat-free chicken broth
- ⅓ cup tomato sauce
- ⅛ teaspoon garlic powder
- ⅛ teaspoon fennel seed
- ⅛ teaspoon onion powder
- 2½ cups cooked pasta

Garnish
- 1 teaspoon chopped fresh parsley
- ¼ cup fresh grated Parmesan cheese

Spray small skillet with nonstick cooking spray. Add pieces of turkey sausage, and brown until all pink is gone.

In small saucepan combine soup and chicken broth. Use a whisk to mix and then add all remaining ingredients.

Add cooked sausage to sauce mixture and simmer over low heat for 5 to 8 minutes.

Garnish sauce with fresh chopped parsley and grated Parmesan, and pour sauce over cooked pasta.

Each serving provides:

228	Calories	5.53 g	Fat
10.97 g	Protein	1073 g	Sodium
32.60 g	Carbohydrate	18.40 mg	Cholesterol

Diabetic exchanges: Med. fat meat, 1; starch, 1½

Spinach Sauce for Pasta

SERVES 4

1½ cups fat-free chicken broth
 2 teaspoons dry onion flakes
 1 clove garlic, pressed
 1 can (14½ ounces) chopped tomatoes
    Dash of red pepper flakes
    Salt and black pepper to taste
⅓ cup frozen chopped spinach, thawed and drained
3½ cups cooked thin spaghetti

In medium saucepan, combine chicken broth, onion flakes, garlic, chopped tomatoes, red pepper flakes, and salt and black pepper to taste. Simmer mixture for 10 to 12 minutes. Add spinach and cook 2 to 3 minutes. Serve over spaghetti.

Each serving provides:

207	Calories	1.10 g	Fat
8.23 g	Protein	668 g	Sodium
41.70 g	Carbohydrate	.0 mg	Cholesterol

Diabetic exchanges: Very lean meat, ½; vegetable, 1; starch, 2

Cherry Pepper and Olive Spread for Sandwiches

SERVES 4

2   mild cherry peppers, stemmed and drained
½   cup fat-free cream cheese
2   tablespoons chopped salad olives, drained
1   clove garlic, pressed
    Dash of seasoned salt (optional)

Chop cherry peppers into small pieces.

Place cream cheese in medium bowl and cream until smooth with an electric mixer. Add all remaining ingredients and mix with mixer.

Use as a zesty spread for sandwiches or as a party dip with crackers. If using as a dip, you might want to double the recipe.

Each serving provides:

36	Calories	.33 g	Fat
5.25 g	Protein	262 g	Sodium
2.61 g	Carbohydrate	2.64 mg	Cholesterol

Diabetic exchanges: Very lean meat, ½; vegetable, 1

Scallops with Cream Sauce

1 small onion, chopped
1 clove garlic, pressed
¼ pound small scallops*
¼ cup white cooking wine
¾ cup fat-free chicken broth
1 teaspoon Molly McButter butter sprinkles
¾ cup skim milk
¼ teaspoon dry thyme
Salt and black pepper to taste
½ cup fat-free sour cream
3 cups cooked linguine
¼ cup shredded Parmesan cheese, for garnish

Thickening
2 tablespoons all-purpose flour
¼ cup skim milk

*If you can't find small scallops, cut larger ones into small pieces.

Spray medium saucepan with nonstick cooking spray. Add onion and garlic. Stir and brown lightly over medium-low heat. Add scallops and cooking wine. Cook and stir 3 to 4 minutes, or until scallops turn white and are done.

Add all remaining ingredients (except sour cream, linguine, and Parmesan) and cook 3 to 4 minutes on low heat.

Combine thickening ingredients with sour cream. Whisk in sour cream mixture and continue stirring over medium heat until sauce thickens. Serve over linguine. Garnish with shredded Parmesan cheese.

Each serving provides:

280	Calories	2.64 g	Fat
17.16 g	Protein	423 g	Sodium
43.29 g	Carbohydrate	14.33 mg	Cholesterol

Diabetic exchanges: Very lean meat, 2; vegetable, 1; starch, 2; skim milk, ¼

DIPS, SAUCES, AND SPREADS

Mushroom Pasta Sauce

4 cups fresh sliced mushrooms
¼ cup fat-free sour cream
1 cup fat-free chicken broth
1 teaspoon dry onion flakes
1 clove garlic, pressed
2 teaspoons Molly McButter butter sprinkles
½ cup Campbell's 98 percent fat-free
   cream of mushroom soup
   Black pepper to taste
3 cups cooked pasta (of your choice)

Spray large skillet with nonstick cooking spray. Add sliced mushrooms and simmer over low heat, covered, for 10 to 15 minutes. Stir occasionally.

In medium bowl, combine sour cream, chicken broth, onion flakes, garlic, Molly McButter, and soup. Use a whisk to blend mixture until smooth. Add black pepper to taste.

Pour soup mixture in skillet with mushrooms and stir with lid off. Stir and cook over medium heat for about 5 minutes. Serve warm over desired pasta.

Each serving provides:

203	Calories	1.76 g	Fat
8.35 g	Protein	559 g	Sodium
38.41 g	Carbohydrate	.75 mg	Cholesterol

Diabetic exchanges: Very lean meat, 1; starch, 2

Creamy Spinach Sauce for Pasta

SERVES 2

½ cup fat-free cream cheese
½ cup fat-free chicken broth
2 tablespoons frozen chopped spinach, thawed,
   drained, and pressed
½ teaspoon dry onion flakes
⅛ teaspoon onion powder
⅛ teaspoon garlic powder
1 tablespoon white cooking wine
½ teaspoon Molly McButter butter sprinkles
⅛ teaspoon black pepper
1½ cups cooked pasta
2 tablespoons shredded Parmesan cheese, for garnish

In small bowl, mix cream cheese with electric mixer until smooth. Gradually add chicken broth and stir with spoon. Add all remaining sauce ingredients. Pour in small saucepan and stir over medium heat until mixture comes to a boil. Reduce heat and stir for 4 to 5 minutes. Serve over pasta.

Garnish each serving with shredded Parmesan.

Each serving provides:

246	Calories	2.23 g	Fat
18.08 g	Protein	762 g	Sodium
36.10 g	Carbohydrate	9.28 mg	Cholesterol

Diabetic exchanges: Very lean meat, 2; vegetable, ½; starch, 2

Alice's Special Pasta Sauce

SERVES 4

1 teaspoon minced garlic
2 tablespoons white cooking wine
⅓ cup white cooking wine
1 cup fresh sliced mushrooms
½ cup chopped canned artichoke hearts
2 tablespoons diced sun-dried tomatoes
2 tablespoons diced roasted bell peppers
1 cup chicken broth
1 tablespoon light sour cream
3 cups pasta (of your choice)
4 tablespoons shredded Parmesan cheese
4 tablespoons toasted pine nuts*

*To toast pine nuts, spray small skillet with nonstick cooking spray. Add pine nuts and brown over low heat. Stir occasionally. Watch carefully, as these burn easily.

Spray medium-large skillet with nonstick cooking spray. Add garlic and 2 tablespoons wine and sauté over medium heat for 2 minutes. Stir while cooking. Next add the ⅓ cup white wine and simmer for 5 minutes. Add mushrooms, artichoke hearts, sun-dried tomatoes, roasted bell peppers, and chicken broth. Simmer for 10 minutes. Stir in sour cream. Serve over desired pasta. Top each serving with a small amount of shredded Parmesan and toasted pine nuts.

Each serving provides:

273	Calories	7.92 g	Fat
11.50 g	Protein	589 g	Sodium
36.54 g	Carbohydrate	5.50 mg	Cholesterol

Diabetic exchanges: Very lean meat, 1; veg., 1; starch, 2; fat, 1

Zucchini and Mushroom Dip

SERVES 6

1½ cups fresh sliced mushrooms
2 small zucchini, cut in small cubes
½ small onion, chopped
1 can (10¾ ounces) Campbell's 98 percent fat-free cream of mushroom soup
1 cup fat-free chicken broth
⅓ cup fat-free sour cream
½ teaspoon Molly McButter butter sprinkles
Dash of garlic salt
Black pepper to taste
4¾ cups cooked spaghetti

Spray large skillet with nonstick cooking spray. Add mushrooms, zucchini, and onion, and cook over medium heat for 10 to 12 minutes, or until vegetables are tender.

In medium bowl, combine soup with chicken broth and sour cream. Use a whisk to blend until smooth. Pour soup mixture over zucchinis and mushrooms in skillet. Add Molly McButter. Simmer for 5 to 8 minutes. Add garlic salt and black pepper and stir. Serve over cooked spaghetti.

Each serving provides:

216	Calories	2.19 g	Fat
8.19 g	Protein	544 g	Sodium
40.56 g	Carbohydrate	1.27 mg	Cholesterol

Diabetic exchanges: Very lean meat, 1; vegetable, 1; starch, 2

White Clam Sauce for Pasta

SERVES 4

1 can (10 ounces) baby clams, drained and rinsed
½ cup skim milk
½ cup fat-free chicken broth
½ small onion, finely chopped
1 clove garlic, pressed
¼ cup fat-free Parmesan cheese
2 teaspoons Molly McButter butter sprinkles
½ teaspoon parsley flakes
Salt and black pepper to taste
1 tablespoon cornstarch
¼ cup fat-free sour cream
2 cups cooked pasta

In small saucepan, combine baby clams, skim milk, chicken broth, onion, and garlic. Simmer over low heat until onions are done. Next, add Parmesan cheese, Molly McButter, parsley, and salt and black pepper to taste.

Remove a small amount of liquid from saucepan and mix with cornstarch and stir to make a thin paste. Pour this mixture back into saucepan and stir until sauce thickens slightly. Whisk in sour cream and serve over pasta.

Each serving provides:

212	Calories	1.26 g	Fat
15.96 g	Protein	346 g	Sodium
31.83 g	Carbohydrate	27.20 mg	Cholesterol

Diabetic exchanges: Very lean meat, 2; vegetable, 1; starch, 1½

Creamy Garlic and Shrimp Sauce for Pasta

SERVES 6

2 cups fat-free chicken broth
4 cloves garlic, pressed
½ teaspoon dry onion flakes
2 tablespoons Molly McButter butter sprinkles
½ cup fat-free sour cream
¼ cup marsala cooking wine
   (available at most supermarkets)
⅛ teaspoon Worcestershire sauce
   Black pepper to taste
12 medium shrimp, peeled and cooked
4½ cups cooked pasta (of your choice)

Thickening
¼ cup water
2 tablespoons flour

In medium saucepan, combine all ingredients for sauce except shrimp and stir over medium heat until well blended. Simmer for about 10 minutes. Stir often.

In small bowl, combine ingredients for sauce thickening and stir until smooth. Stir this mixture into sauce mixture and stir over low heat until sauce starts to thicken. Note that this is a thin sauce, so it is not going to thicken a great deal.

Add shrimp and simmer 1 to 2 minutes. Serve warm over desired pasta.

Each serving provides:

218	Calories	1.01 g	Fat
12.76 g	Protein	644 g	Sodium
37.66 g	Carbohydrate	49.18 mg	Cholesterol

Diabetic exchanges: Very lean meat, 1; vegetable, 1; starch, 2

Veggie Sauce for Linguine

SERVES 2

1¼ cups fat-free chicken broth
 1 can (14½ ounces) chopped tomatoes
 1 carrot, sliced
 1 stalk celery, thinly sliced
 1 clove garlic, pressed
 1 small onion, chopped
    Salt and black pepper to taste
 ½ teaspoon Molly McButter butter sprinkles
1½ cups cooked linguine
 4 tablespoons shredded Parmesan cheese, for garnish

In medium saucepan, combine chicken broth and chopped tomatoes. Cook over medium heat while adding carrot, celery, garlic, and onion. Bring to a slow boil, reduce heat, and simmer for about 15 minutes. Add salt, black pepper, and Molly McButter. Serve over cooked linguini.

Garnish with Parmesan cheese.

Each serving provides:

290	Calories	4.42 g	Fat
13.78 g	Protein	1444 g	Sodium
50.55 g	Carbohydrate	8.0 mg	Cholesterol

Diabetic exchanges: Lean meat, 1; vegetable, 3; starch, 2

Tomato and Basil Sauce for Pasta

SERVES 4

1   small onion, chopped
1   cup fresh sliced mushrooms
2   cloves garlic, pressed
1   can (14½ ounces) chopped tomatoes
2   cups fat-free chicken broth
¼   cup fresh chopped basil
⅛   teaspoon oregano
2   tablespoons white cooking wine
    Salt and black pepper to taste
3   cups cooked pasta (of your choice)
4   tablespoons shredded Parmesan, for garnish
3   cups cooked pasta

Spray medium saucepan with nonstick cooking spray. Add onion, mushrooms, and garlic. Cook over low heat until mushrooms are done. Add all remaining ingredients except Parmesan and continue to simmer for 12 to 15 minutes. Serve over pasta, garnish with Parmesan, and enjoy.

Each serving provides:

225	Calories	2.60 g	Fat
10.03 g	Protein	919 g	Sodium
39.51 g	Carbohydrate	4.0 mg	Cholesterol

Diabetic exchanges: Med. fat meat, ½; vegetable, 1; starch, 2

2

Soups, Salads, and Appetizers

Ravioli Soup

½ link sweet Italian turkey sausage
1 small onion, chopped
1 stalk celery, chopped
2 cups water
2½ cups fat-free chicken broth
1 clove garlic, pressed
1 cup refrigerated-type cheese ravioli
¼ teaspoon Italian seasoning
　Dash of red pepper flakes
　Salt and black pepper to taste

Spray large pot with nonstick cooking spray. Add sausage pieces, onion, and celery. Brown over medium heat. Add all remaining ingredients and simmer for 35 to 45 minutes over very low heat.

Each serving provides:

108	Calories	2.13 g	Fat
7.87 g	Protein	906 g	Sodium
14.63 g	Carbohydrate	6.25 mg	Cholesterol

Diabetic exchanges: Lean meat, ¾; vegetable, 1; starch, ½

Savory Soup

1 small onion, chopped
2 cloves garlic, pressed
½ cup sliced carrots
1 can (14½ ounces) diced tomatoes (use the juice)
½ cup canned small white beans
½ cup canned kidney beans (white or red)
½ cup canned peas
½ cup red cooking wine
2 cups fat-free chicken broth
½ cup water
⅛ teaspoon savory
⅛ teaspoon thyme
Salt and black pepper to taste
½ cup dry pasta (reserve for end of cooking)

Mix all ingredients together, except dry pasta, in large cooking pot. Simmer, covered, over medium-low heat for 1 to 2 hours. Add dry pasta and continue cooking until pasta is done.

Each serving provides:

133	Calories	.56 g	Fat
6.26 g	Protein	829 g	Sodium
23.42 g	Carbohydrate	0 mg	Cholesterol

Diabetic exchanges: Vegetable, 2; starch, 1

Pasta Soup with Ground Beef

¼ pound extra-lean ground beef
2 cups water
1 can (14 ounces) beef broth, remove fat
1 can (14½ ounces) stewed tomatoes
½ cup tomato sauce
1 clove garlic, pressed
2 teaspoons dry ranch dressing mix
2 teaspoons dry onion flakes
2 teaspoons packaged dry spaghetti sauce mix
½ cup sliced carrots
½ teaspoon dry celery flakes
   Salt and black pepper to taste
½ cup uncooked pasta

Spray large pot with nonstick cooking spray. Brown ground beef, then add all remaining ingredients, except pasta. Cook and simmer until carrots are done.

Add pasta and cook only until pasta is done, about 10 to 12 minutes.

Serve warm. Great with a tossed salad and lowfat garlic toast.

Each serving provides:

109	Calories	2.63 g	Fat
6.76 g	Protein	808 g	Sodium
15.0 g	Carbohydrate	11.71 mg	Cholesterol

Diabetic exchanges: Lean meat, 1; vegetable, ½; starch, ½

Minestrone Soup

⅓ cup canned kidney beans
⅓ cup dry lentils, washed
2 cloves garlic, pressed
3 cans (14½ ounces each) fat-free chicken broth
3 cups water
1 can (14½ ounces) chopped stewed tomatoes
1 medium onion, chopped
¾ cup sliced carrots
1 cup sliced cabbage
¾ cup dry uncooked elbow macaroni
⅛ teaspoon oregano flakes
  Salt and black pepper to taste
1 link sweet Italian turkey sausage, sliced and browned
  Shredded Parmesan cheese, for garnish

Combine all ingredients, except sausage, in large pot and cook until liquid comes to a boil. Reduce heat and simmer. After reducing heat, spray small skillet with nonstick cooking spray and brown pieces of turkey sausage. When browned, add to soup mixture. Simmer for 1 to 1½ hours. Serve warm with Parmesan cheese as a garnish on each serving, if desired.

Each serving provides:

171	Calories	1.69 g	Fat
11.21 g	Protein	1265 g	Sodium
29.02 g	Carbohydrate	13.17 mg	Cholesterol

Diabetic exchanges: Lean meat, 1; vegetable, 1½; starch, 1

Meatball Soup

Soup
4   cups fat-free chicken broth
2   cups water
1   can (14½ ounces) chopped tomatoes
2   cloves garlic, pressed
1   medium onion, chopped
⅛   teaspoon dry oregano flakes
⅛   teaspoon onion powder
1   cup sliced carrots
1   cup fresh sliced mushrooms
½   stalk celery, sliced
    Salt and black pepper to taste

Meatballs
¼   pound ground turkey breast
¼   cup crushed fat-free soda crackers
2   tablespoons fat-free liquid egg product
2   tablespoons finely chopped onion
1   clove garlic
    Salt and black pepper to taste

SOUPS, SALADS, AND APPETIZERS

Use a large pot and combine all ingredients for soup. Bring to a boil, then lower heat to simmer. Cook, covered, for 35 to 40 minutes.

In medium bowl, combine all ingredients for meatballs. Mix thoroughly. Form meat mixture into walnut-sized balls. Spray skillet with nonstick cooking spray. Add meatballs and brown them on all sides. Add meatballs to soup and simmer for about 20 minutes. Serve with some wonderful hot garlic bread.

Each serving provides:

69	Calories	.47	g	Fat
6.30 g	Protein	695	g	Sodium
10.31 g	Carbohydrate	8.51	mg	Cholesterol

Diabetic exchanges: Very lean meat, 1; vegetable, 1

Italian Sausage Bean Soup

1   cup small white dry beans, cleaned and rinsed
½   cup dry lentils, cleaned and rinsed
6   cups water
1   can (14½ ounces) fat-free chicken broth
1   link sweet Italian turkey sausage, sliced or cut in chunks
1   small onion, chopped
2   cloves garlic, pressed
1   can (14½ ounces) stewed tomatoes
¼   teaspoon onion powder
½   teaspoon Italian seasoning
¼   teaspoon red pepper flakes
⅛   teaspoon fennel seeds
¼   teaspoon seasoned salt
    Black pepper to taste

In large pot, combine white beans, lentils, water, and chicken broth. Bring to a boil, then reduce heat and simmer for 1 hour, covered. Stir occasionally.

Spray small skillet with nonstick cooking spray, add pieces of turkey sausage, and brown until all pink is gone.

After beans have cooked for 1 hour, add all remaining ingredients including sausage and simmer for 30 to 45 minutes longer. Great served with garlic toast.

Each serving provides:

218	Calories	1.61 g	Fat
16.33 g	Protein	642 g	Sodium
36.75 g	Carbohydrate	8.33 mg	Cholesterol

Diabetic exchanges: Very lean meat, 1; vegetable, 1; starch, 2

Cream of Broccoli and Potato Soup

2 cups chicken broth
1 small potato, cut into small cubes
½ small onion, chopped
1 clove garlic, pressed
1 cup water
1 teaspoon Molly McButter butter sprinkles
1 cup broccoli florets, cut into small pieces
1 cup skim milk
⅓ cup fat-free sour cream
  Salt and black pepper to taste

In medium saucepan, combine chicken broth, potato pieces, onion, garlic, water, and Molly McButter. Simmer over medium heat until potatoes and onions are done. Add broccoli pieces and simmer about another 10 minutes, or until broccoli is tender. Add milk, and using a whisk, stir in sour cream. Add salt and black pepper to taste. Simmer and stir for 2 to 3 minutes. Do not boil. Remove from heat and serve.

Each serving provides:

76	Calories	.24 g	Fat
5.87 g	Protein	596 g	Sodium
13.05 g	Carbohydrate	1.0 mg	Cholesterol

Diabetic exchanges: Vegetable, 1; starch, ⅓; skim milk, ¼

Cream of Spinach Soup

SERVES 4

1 small onion, chopped
1 clove garlic, pressed
½ cup frozen chopped spinach, thawed and drained
1½ cups chicken broth
1 teaspoon Molly McButter butter sprinkles
Salt and black pepper to taste
2 cups skim milk
½ cup fat-free sour cream

Spray medium saucepan with nonstick cooking spray. Add onion and garlic and simmer until onion is tender. Add all ingredients, except milk and sour cream, and simmer over low heat for 8 to 10 minutes.

In medium bowl, whisk together milk and sour cream. When smooth, add this mixture to spinach mixture. Simmer over low heat for about 5 minutes. Serve warm.

Each serving provides:

91	Calories	.34 g	Fat
8.16 g	Protein	521 g	Sodium
14.12 g	Carbohydrate	2.0 mg	Cholesterol

Diabetic exchanges: Vegetable, 2; skim milk, ½

Onion Soup

2 medium onions, thinly sliced
2 cans (14½ ounces each) fat-free chicken broth
½ teaspoon celery flakes
1 clove garlic, pressed
¼ teaspoon onion powder
1 tablespoon Molly McButter butter sprinkles
   Salt and black pepper to taste

Garnish
1 tablespoon fresh chopped parsley
¼ cup fat-free grated mozzarella cheese

Simmer all ingredients for soup in medium saucepan. Cook until onion is done.

Serve hot in bowls. Garnish top of soup with parsley and grated cheese.

Each serving provides:

62	Calories	.23 g	Fat
5.28 g	Protein	1086 g	Sodium
9.97 g	Carbohydrate	1.25 mg	Cholesterol

Diabetic exchanges: Lean meat, ½; vegetable, 1½

Winter Soup

SERVES 8

1 link sweet Italian turkey sausage, cut into small slices
2 cans (14½ ounces each) fat-free chicken broth
1 small onion, chopped
1 can (4 ounces) sliced mushrooms, drained
1 cup stewed tomatoes
1 can (14½ ounces) cut green beans, drained
1 cup sliced carrots
1 clove garlic, pressed
½ teaspoon dry celery flakes
⅛ teaspoon red pepper flakes
   Dash of oregano
⅛ teaspoon onion powder
1 cup water
   Garlic salt to taste
   Black pepper to taste
   Dash of seasoned salt
⅓ cup small elbow macaroni

Spray large saucepan with nonstick cooking spray and brown sliced sausage. Add all remaining ingredients, except macaroni, and simmer for about an hour. Add pasta and cook 12 to 15 more minutes.

Serve warm. (It's wonderful warmed and eaten the next day also.)

Each serving provides:

75	Calories	1.04 g	Fat
4.84 g	Protein	841 g	Sodium
12.24 g	Carbohydrate	6.25 mg	Cholesterol

Diabetic exchanges: Very lean meat, ¼; vegetable, 2; starch, ¼

Vegetable Stew with Fennel

SERVES 6

    1   small onion, chopped
    1   cup fresh sliced mushrooms
    1   stalk celery, sliced
    1   cup sliced carrots
    2   cups sliced cabbage
 2½   cups fat-free chicken broth
    3   cups water
    1   small potato, peeled and cut into small cubes
    1   can (14½ ounces) chopped tomatoes
  ½   teaspoon fennel seed, lightly crushed
  ⅛   teaspoon oregano
        Salt to taste

Spray large pot with nonstick cooking spray. Add onion, mushrooms, and celery, and simmer over low heat until soft, about 10 to 12 minutes. Add all remaining ingredients and simmer for 1 hour. Great served with garlic toast.

Each serving provides:

58	Calories	.38 g	Fat
2.89 g	Protein	622 g	Sodium
12.31 g	Carbohydrate	0 mg	Cholesterol

Diabetic exchanges: Vegetable, 1½; starch, ¼

Bean and Pasta Soup

¾ cup small white dry beans, rinsed
3 cups water
1 can (14½ ounces) fat-free chicken broth
1 small onion, chopped
2 cloves garlic, pressed
1 can (14½ ounces) stewed tomatoes
½ teaspoon celery flakes
½ teaspoon Italian seasoning
¼ teaspoon red pepper flakes
¾ cup elbow macaroni, uncooked

In a large pot, cook beans, water, and chicken broth over medium heat for 1 hour. Add all remaining ingredients, except macaroni, and simmer for about ½ hour longer. Add macaroni and cook for about 15 minutes longer.

Serve warm.

Each serving provides:

166	Calories	.61 g	Fat
9.20 g	Protein	483 g	Sodium
32.16 g	Carbohydrate	0 mg	Cholesterol

Diabetic exchanges: Vegetable, 2; starch, 1½

Vegetable and Ravioli Soup

SERVES 6

1 cup sliced carrots
1 medium onion, chopped
2 cloves garlic, pressed
1 medium potato, peeled and cut into small cubes
1 can (14½ ounces) fat-free chicken broth
1 can (15 ounces) tomato sauce
1 cup sliced fresh mushrooms
½ teaspoon Molly McButter butter sprinkles
½ teaspoon Italian seasoning
1 cup water
   Salt and black pepper to taste
1 cup refrigerated-type lowfat cheese ravioli

Place all ingredients, except ravioli, in large saucepan and simmer over medium heat until potatoes and carrots are done, about 15 minutes. Increase heat to medium-high and add ravioli. Cook another 7 to 8 minutes. Serve warm.

Each serving provides:

123	Calories	1.44 g	Fat
6.59 g	Protein	905 g	Sodium
23.05 g	Carbohydrate	0 mg	Cholesterol

Diabetic exchanges: Vegetable, 2; starch, 1

Tortellini Chicken Soup

SERVES 6

1 small onion, chopped
1 boneless, skinless chicken breast (3 ounces),
  cut into small pieces
1 clove garlic, pressed
2 cups water
2 cans (14½ ounces each) fat-free chicken broth
¾ cup sliced carrots
1 cup fresh sliced mushrooms
¼ cup sliced celery
1 teaspoon Molly McButter butter sprinkles
¼ teaspoon Italian seasoning
⅛ teaspoon red pepper flakes
  Garlic salt to taste
¾ cup packaged fresh cheese tortellini

Spray large pot with nonstick cooking spray. Add onion, chicken, and garlic, and brown over medium heat. Add all remaining ingredients, except tortellini. Bring soup to a boil, then reduce heat to low. Cover and cook for about 1 hour. Add tortellini and cook for recommended time on package. Serve warm.

Each serving provides:

91	Calories	1.54 g	Fat
7.53 g	Protein	683 g	Sodium
12.04 g	Carbohydrate	25.40 mg	Cholesterol

Diabetic exchanges: Lean meat, ½; vegetable, 1; starch, ½

Veggie and Pasta Soup

SERVES 8

½ cup dry kidney beans, washed and soaked overnight
½ cup uncooked elbow macaroni
3 cups fat-free chicken broth
3 cups water
1 medium onion, chopped
2 cloves garlic, pressed
1 stalk celery, sliced
½ cup sliced carrots
1 small zucchini, peeled and cut into small cubes
2 teaspoons Molly McButter butter sprinkles
⅛ teaspoon oregano
⅛ teaspoon onion powder
   Pinch of fennel seed
   Dash of crushed red pepper
   Salt and black pepper to taste

Rinse soaked beans and drain. Combine beans in large pot with all other ingredients, except macaroni. Bring to a boil, then lower heat to simmer and cook for 1 hour. Check beans for doneness. If beans are tender and cooked through, add the macaroni and cook for 8 to 10 minutes. When macaroni is done, remove from heat and serve.

Each serving provides:

87	Calories	.31 g	Fat
5.06 g	Protein	431 g	Sodium
16.43 g	Carbohydrate	0 mg	Cholesterol

Diabetic exchanges: Vegetable, 2; starch, ½

Spaghetti Salad with Chicken

1 cooked, boneless, skinless chicken breast (3 ounces)
½ teaspoon dry Good Seasons Gourmet Caesar salad
   dressing mix
¼ cup fat-free Italian salad dressing
4½ cups cooked spaghetti
1 medium tomato, chopped
1 cup fresh spinach leaves
   Garlic salt to taste
1 tablespoon shredded Parmesan cheese

Cut cooked chicken breast into small pieces. Mix dry Caesar
salad dressing mix with the Italian dressing. Mix and toss
together with all remaining ingredients in large bowl. Serve
and enjoy.

Each serving provides:

189	Calories	1.56 g	Fat
10.19 g	Protein	300 g	Sodium
32.51 g	Carbohydrate	12.70 mg	Cholesterol

Diabetic exchanges: Very lean meat, ½; vegetable, ½; starch, 2

Shell Pasta Salad

½ cup sliced carrots, lightly steamed
½ cup chopped broccoli, lightly steamed
2 cups cooked medium-sized shell pasta
2 slices turkey bacon, cooked and crumbled
½ cup frozen peas, thawed
1 small purple onion, chopped
1 stalk celery, sliced
¼ teaspoon garlic salt
  Dash of seasoned salt
½ cup fat-free ranch salad dressing

Lightly steam carrots and broccoli. Combine all ingredients for salad, except dressing. Toss and mix. Add salad dressing and chill.

Each serving provides:

206	Calories	1.38 g	Fat
6.93 g	Protein	613 g	Sodium
40.10 g	Carbohydrate	5.0 mg	Cholesterol

Diabetic exchanges: Vegetable, 2; starch, 2

Seafood Pasta Salad

¾ cup sliced carrots
¼ pound imitation crab meat, cut into small pieces
3 cups cooked pasta spirals
2 green onions, chopped
1 teaspoon fresh chopped parsley
½ teaspoon dry dill weed
¼ cup shredded Parmesan cheese
1 medium tomato, chopped
⅛ teaspoon oregano flakes
   Salt and black pepper to taste

Dressing
⅓ cup fat-free Miracle Whip
1 teaspoon red wine vinegar

Steam or cook carrots until slightly tender. Do not fully cook. Remove from heat and rinse with cold water and drain.

In large bowl, combine all ingredients for salad and toss.

In small bowl, combine ingredients for dressing. Mix thoroughly.

Add dressing to salad and mix. Chill for 30 minutes to 1 hour and serve.

Each serving provides:

227	Calories	2.70 g	Fat
11.47 g	Protein	511 g	Sodium
39.15 g	Carbohydrate	9.67 mg	Cholesterol

Diabetic exchanges: Lean meat, 1; vegetable, ½; starch, 2

Fettucine Salad

SERVES 3

2 tablespoons lemon juice
½ cup fat-free mayonnaise
1½ cups cooked fettucine
2 green onions, sliced
½ cup fresh sliced mushrooms
½ cup chopped green pepper
1 boiled egg white, chopped (discard yolk)
4 tablespoons fancy grated Parmesan cheese
  Dash of cayenne pepper
  Garlic salt to taste
  Black pepper to taste

In small bowl, combine lemon juice with fat-free mayonnaise and mix with spoon. In large bowl, combine all ingredients for salad. Add dressing and toss. Chill and serve.

Each serving provides:

175	Calories	2.55 g	Fat
7.81 g	Protein	464 g	Sodium
29.66 g	Carbohydrate	5.33 mg	Cholesterol

Diabetic exchanges: Lean meat, 1; vegetable, 1; starch, 1½

Mandarin Orange Salad

4 cups tossed lettuce and salad greens
1 small purple onion, sliced
½ cup mandarin orange pieces
¼ green or yellow bell pepper, sliced in long slivers
¼ teaspoon poppy seeds
¼ cup fat-free zesty Italian dressing

Combine all ingredients for salad, except dressing, in large bowl and toss. Chill lightly. Add dressing and serve.

Each serving provides:

46	Calories	.25 g	Fat
1.19 g	Protein	227 g	Sodium
9.62 g	Carbohydrate	0 mg	Cholesterol

Diabetic exchanges: Vegetable, ½; fruit, ½

Pepperoni Pasta Salad

SERVES 4

2½ cups cooked tricolored pasta spirals
1 small onion, chopped
8 pieces Hormel turkey pepperoni, cut into small pieces
1 medium tomato, cut into small chunks
½ medium cucumber, chopped
⅓ cup chopped fresh green or red bell pepper
¼ cup shredded Parmesan cheese
  Garlic salt and black pepper to taste
½ cup fat-free ranch or Italian dressing

In large bowl, combine all ingredients. Chill for 30 to 45 minutes. Then mix and serve.

Each serving provides:

232	Calories	2.79 g	Fat
8.24 g	Protein	512 g	Sodium
41.90 g	Carbohydrate	8.71 mg	Cholesterol

Diabetic exchanges: Lean meat, 1; vegetable, 2; starch, 1½

Zesty Salad with Parmesan

4 cups assorted lettuce and salad greens
6 cherry tomatoes, cut in half
1 small purple onion, sliced
4 tablespoons fat-free Italian dressing
½ cup fat-free salad croutons
4 tablespoons fancy shredded Parmesan cheese

In large bowl, combine all ingredients for salad, except Parmesan cheese and croutons, and toss. Add dressing and croutons just before serving. Garnish top of salad with Parmesan cheese.

Each serving provides:

75	Calories	1.77 g	Fat
3.26 g	Protein	330 g	Sodium
10.96 g	Carbohydrate	4.0 mg	Cholesterol

Diabetic exchanges: Lean meat, ½; vegetable, 2

Pasta Salad with Raspberry Vinaigrette

SERVES 8

Salad

4   cups cooked pasta, rinsed with cool water
3   green onions, sliced
1   clove garlic, pressed
¼   cup green pepper, chopped
½   cup frozen corn
½   cup frozen baby peas
¾   cup water packed artichoke hearts, quartered
1   tablespoon fresh parsley, chopped

Dressing

½   cup raspberry balsamic vinegar
2   teaspoons light olive oil
2   teaspoons toasted sesame seeds

Combine cooked pasta and all other salad ingredients and toss.

In a small bowl, combine ingredients for dressing and mix thoroughly. Pour dressing over salad and toss and mix. Chill for at least 1 hour before serving.

Each serving provides:

154	Calories	2.14 g	Fat
4.80 g	Protein	61.02 g	Sodium
28.88 g	Carbohydrate	0 mg	Cholesterol

Diabetic exchanges: Vegetable, 1; starch, 1; fat, 1

Lemon Garlic Pasta Salad

2 cups cooked spiral pasta
1 cup sliced carrots, lightly steamed or partially cooked
1 medium cucumber, chopped
3 green onions, sliced
1 large tomato, cut into small chunks
2 tablespoons fat-free Parmesan cheese
   Black pepper to taste
   Garlic salt to taste

Dressing
½ cup fat-free mayonnaise
1½ tablespoons fresh lemon juice
1 clove garlic, pressed
   Dash of seasoned salt

Garnish
2 tablespoons shredded Parmesan

Combine all ingredients for dressing in small bowl and stir until smooth.

In large bowl, combine all ingredients for salad and mix with large spoon. Add dressing mixture and stir. Chill for at least 1 hour before serving. Sprinkle a little shredded Parmesan on top of salad when serving.

Each serving provides:

119	Calories	1.01 g	Fat
4.09 g	Protein	225 g	Saturated fat
23.36 g	Carbohydrate	2.33 mg	Cholesterol

Diabetic exchanges: Lean meat, ¼; vegetable, 1; starch, 1

Pasta Salad with Toasted Pine Nuts

SERVES 4

3 cups cooked tricolored pasta spirals
½ small onion, chopped
1 cup sliced carrots, lightly steamed
½ cup water packed artichoke hearts, cut into quarters
  Garlic salt to taste
  Black pepper to taste

Dressing
2 teaspoons sesame seeds, toasted
2 tablespoons pine nuts, lightly chopped and toasted
½ cup "Alessi" white balsamic raspberry blush vinegar
2 teaspoons light olive oil
1 clove garlic, pressed

In large bowl, combine all ingredients for salad and mix. Set aside.

Spray small skillet with nonstick cooking spray. Add sesame seeds and pine nuts and brown over low heat. Watch carefully, as these burn quickly.

In small bowl, combine toasted seeds and pine nuts with remaining ingredients for dressing. Mix thoroughly. Pour dressing evenly over pasta salad and stir. Cover and chill for at least 1 hour. Stir occasionally while chilling. Serve cold.

Each serving provides:

263	Calories	6.49 g	Fat
7.54 g	Protein	82.78 g	Sodium
44.21 g	Carbohydrate	0 mg	Cholesterol

Diabetic exchanges: Vegetable, 1; starch, 2; fat, 1½

Penne Pasta Salad

2 cups frozen "Birds Eye" baby corn–blend vegetables
2 cups cooked penne pasta
½ small onion, finely chopped
¼ cup fat-free zesty Italian salad dressing (or any favorite fat-free dressing)
2 tablespoons salad olives, drained
½ cup water-packed artichoke hearts, quartered and drained
  Black pepper to taste (I like plenty)
  Garlic salt to taste

Combine all ingredients for salad. Toss and mix and set aside until frozen vegetables are thawed. Store in refrigerator until ready to serve.

Each serving provides:

143	Calories	1.08 g	Fat
5.15 g	Protein	517 g	Sodium
27.68 g	Carbohydrate	0 mg	Cholesterol

Diabetic exchanges: Very lean meat, ½; vegetable, 2; starch, 1

Cottage Cheese and Pasta Salad

SERVES 4

2   cups cooked tricolored pasta spirals
¾   cup 1 percent cottage cheese
¾   cup carrots, lightly steamed
3   green onions, chopped
¼   cup shredded Parmesan cheese
½   cup Kraft shredded fat-free mozzarella cheese
2   tablespoons fat-free ranch dressing
    Garlic salt to taste
    Black pepper to taste

Combine all ingredients in large bowl and mix gently. Chill
for 30 to 45 minutes. Mix again and serve.

Each serving provides:

202	Calories	2.46 g	Fat
15.66 g	Protein	474 g	Sodium
28.16 g	Carbohydrate	8.38 mg	Cholesterol

Diabetic exchanges: Very lean meat, 2½; vegetable, 1; starch, 1

Garlic Pasta Salad

3 cups cooked pasta spirals
1 small clove garlic, pressed
2 green onions, sliced
¾ cup frozen peas
1 tablespoon capers (optional)
¼ green or red bell pepper, cut into pieces
   Juice from 1 lemon
   Garlic salt to taste
   Black pepper to taste
⅓ cup fat-free mayonnaise
½ cup fat-free cream cheese
1 tablespoon white balsamic vinegar

Combine all ingredients, except mayonnaise, cream cheese, and balsamic vinegar, in large bowl and mix. In food processor, combine mayonnaise and cream cheese and mix until smooth. Pour this dressing over the pasta mixture and stir. Add balsamic vinegar and stir. Chill for an hour or more before serving so the flavors will have time to blend.

Each serving provides:

151	Calories	.55	g	Fat
7.85 g	Protein	233	g	Sodium
27.92 g	Carbohydrate	1.76	mg	Cholesterol

Diabetic exchanges: Very lean meat, ½; vegetable, 1; starch, 1¼

Quick and Easy Onion and Cheese Focaccia

SERVES 6

10 ounces Pillsbury refrigerated pizza dough
 1 cup Healthy Choice lowfat mozzarella shredded cheese
 1 medium onion, thinly sliced
 2 cloves garlic, pressed
    Garlic salt to taste

Preheat oven to 400 degrees.

Remove pizza dough from roll, form into a ball, and knead a few times. Place dough in medium bowl. Add ½ cup of the shredded cheese, and knead cheese into dough. Continue kneading until cheese is mixed into dough fairly well. Set aside.

Spray small skillet with nonstick cooking spray. Add onions and brown over medium heat until onions are tender. Add garlic and stir.

Spray 9-inch round cake pan with nonstick cooking spray. Roll ball of dough out on dry surface. Roll from the center out to make a circle. Roll bigger than the pan, as it shrinks quickly after rolling. Place dough in round pan and spread onions and garlic over the top of dough. Sprinkle on the other ½ cup shredded cheese and a little garlic salt on top, if desired.

Bake at 400 degrees for 20 to 25 minutes, or until golden brown. Cut like a pizza with a pizza cutter.

Each serving provides:

171		Calories	2.72	g	Fat
11.03	g	Protein	260	g	Sodium
24.48	g	Carbohydrate	4.67	mg	Cholesterol

Diabetic exchanges: Lean meat, 1; starch, 1½

Italian Sausage Rolls
with Peppers and Onions

SERVES 2

1 sweet Italian turkey sausage, cut in half lengthwise
½ red bell pepper, sliced in thin strips
1 medium onion, thinly sliced
1 clove garlic
  Salt and black pepper to taste
⅓ cup Kraft shredded fat-free mozzarella
2 lowfat hot dog buns

Spray medium skillet with nonstick cooking spray. Add sausage halves and cook on both sides until done thoroughly. Remove sausage from pan and set aside. Add to pan peppers, onions, garlic, and salt and black pepper to taste. Stir peppers and onions over medium-low heat until they are tender.

Place half of sausage on bun and add peppers, onions, and half the cheese. Repeat with other bun.

Each serving provides:

247	Calories	5.39	g	Fat
17.81 g	Protein	785	g	Sodium
30.44 g	Carbohydrate	28.33	mg	Cholesterol

Diabetic exchanges: Lean meat, 2; vegetable, ½; starch, 1½

Potato and Onion Frittata

½ small onion, chopped
1 small potato, peeled and chopped into small pieces
½ cup fat-free liquid egg product
  Dash of garlic salt or powder
  Salt and black pepper to taste

Spray small skillet with nonstick cooking spray. Add onion and potato and stir over medium-low heat until tender and browned slightly.

Add seasonings to liquid egg product and stir. Pour egg mixture in skillet over potatoes and onions. Do not stir. Cover and simmer over low heat until egg is set. Cut in half and serve.

Each serving provides:

92	Calories	.10 g	Fat
10.29 g	Protein	153 g	Sodium
12.14 g	Carbohydrate	0 mg	Cholesterol

Diabetic exchanges: Very lean meat, 1; vegetable, ½; starch, ½

Golden Polenta with Roasted Pine Nuts

4 slices polenta, ½ inch thick (I buy the kind in a roll at the supermarket.)
3 tablespoons pine nuts, lightly chopped
1 large onion, sliced
1 cup 1 percent cottage cheese
1 teaspoon dry onion flakes
  Garlic salt to taste
  Black pepper to taste
4 tablespoons lowfat red pasta sauce
½ cup Kraft fat-free shredded mozzarella cheese

Preheat oven to 350 degrees.

Spray medium skillet with nonstick cooking spray. Add slices of polenta and brown over medium heat, on each side. While polenta is browning, spray a small skillet with nonstick cooking spray and add pine nuts. Stir and brown over low heat. Watch carefully as these burn easily. Set aside after browning.

Spray another skillet with nonstick cooking spray, add onion, and brown and simmer over very low heat until onion is tender. Set aside.

In small bowl, combine cottage cheese, onion flakes, garlic salt, and black pepper. Mix with spoon.

Spray medium baking dish with nonstick cooking spray (I used a glass pie plate). Line bottom of dish with cottage cheese mixture. Place each slice of browned polenta on cottage cheese. Top each slice of polenta with toasted pine nuts and browned onion. Then add 1 teaspoon pasta sauce on each slice and sprinkle the top of entire dish with shredded mozzarella cheese. Bake at 350 degrees for 15 minutes. Serve warm from the oven.

Each serving provides:

159	Calories	4.59 g	Fat
15.13 g	Protein	533 g	Sodium
15.94 g	Carbohydrate	5.0 mg	Cholesterol

Diabetic exchanges: Lean meat, 1½; starch, ½; fat, 1

Focaccia with Cheese

SERVES 8

1½ cups warm water
1 package (½ ounce) active dry yeast
1 teaspoon sugar
1 teaspoon olive oil
2½ cups flour
2 teaspoons Molly McButter butter sprinkles
½ teaspoon salt
½ cup dry instant potatoes
⅓ cup shredded fat-free mozzarella cheese
Garlic salt to taste
1 teaspoon sesame seeds

Preheat oven to 375 degrees.

In small bowl, combine warm water, yeast, and sugar. Stir until yeast and sugar are dissolved. Add olive oil then set aside.

In large bowl, mix flour, Molly McButter, salt, and potato flakes. Add yeast mixture to flour mixture and mix with a large spoon until thoroughly blended. You might need to add a few tablespoons of water to make the dough moist enough to mix.

After 1 hour, add cheese and mix thoroughly.

Spray 9-inch round pan with nonstick cooking spray. Spread dough into pan and extend to edges. Keep stretching the dough to stay at the edges. Spray top of dough with butter-flavored cooking spray then sprinkle top of dough with garlic salt and sesame seeds. Bake at 375 degrees for 35 to 40 minutes. Cut in pie-shaped pieces like a pizza. Serve with pasta or dips and spreads.

Cuts best with a pizza cutter.

Each serving provides:

156	Calories	1.18 g	Fat
5.75 g	Protein	214 g	Sodium
29.96 g	Carbohydrate	.83 mg	Cholesterol

Diabetic exchanges: Very lean meat, 1; starch, 1½

Garlic Cheese Sticks

¼ cup crushed corn flakes
½ teaspoon Molly McButter butter sprinkles
   Pinch of Italian seasoning
¼ teaspoon garlic powder
¼ cup fat-free liquid egg product
4 pieces Healthy Choice mozzarella string cheese

In small bowl, combine crushed corn flakes, Molly McButter, Italian seasoning, and garlic powder.

Spray small skillet with nonstick cooking spray. Pour egg product in shallow dish. Pour corn flake mixture in plate. Coat each cheese stick with egg product then roll in corn flake mixture. Place each stick in skillet. Heat skillet quickly and brown each cheese stick on each side over medium-high heat for about 1 minute, or until good and brown. Very carefully turn sticks with tongs. When all sides are browned, carefully remove sticks from skillet with tongs and place on paper towel to cool slightly.

Serve warm. These are a big hit as an appetizer.

Each serving provides:

159	Calories	3.19 g	Fat
19.73 g	Protein	640 g	Sodium
12.53 g	Carbohydrate	6.0 mg	Cholesterol

Diabetic exchanges: Very lean meat, 3; starch, ½

Focaccia with Onion

SERVES 8

1¼ cups warm water
2 teaspoons sugar
1 package (¼ ounce) active dry yeast
1 teaspoon olive oil
2 cups all-purpose flour
½ teaspoon salt
2 teaspoons Molly McButter butter sprinkles
¼ cup instant potato flakes
1 large onion, sliced
 Butter-flavored cooking spray
 Garlic salt to taste
1 teaspoon poppy seeds

Preheat oven to 375 degrees.

In small bowl, combine warm water, sugar, and yeast. Stir until yeast and sugar are dissolved. Add olive oil and set aside.

In large bowl, combine flour, salt, Molly McButter, and potato flakes. Add yeast mixture to flour mixture and mix thoroughly. If dough is too dry, add 1 to 3 tablespoons of water. Continue mixing. Cover dough and set in warm place for 1 hour. Dough should double in size.

While dough is rising, spray large skillet with nonstick cooking spray. Add sliced onion and cook over medium heat.

Cover and simmer until almost done. Do not brown onions. These will finish cooking in the oven later. Set aside for topping.

Spray 8- to 9-inch pan with nonstick cooking spray. Remove dough from bowl and spread into pan. Work the dough out toward the edges of the pan. Spray top of dough with butter-flavored cooking spray and arrange cooked onion over top of dough. Sprinkle with garlic salt and poppy seeds.

Bake at 375 degrees for 35 to 40 minutes. Serve warm with pasta or as an appetizer with a dip. Slice like a pizza.

Each serving provides:

145	Calories	1.15 g	Fat
4.09 g	Protein	181 g	Sodium
29.16 g	Carbohydrate	0 mg	Cholesterol

Diabetic exchanges: Vegetable, 1; starch, 1½

Frittata

½ small onion, chopped
1 cup fat-free liquid egg product
1 slice lowfat smoked ham luncheon meat,
  cut into squares
½ teaspoon Molly McButter butter sprinkles
½ cup frozen corn, thawed
  Salt and black pepper to taste
4 tablespoons marinara sauce (optional)

Spray small skillet with nonstick cooking spray and add onion.
Cook and stir onion until tender. Set aside to cool slightly.

In small bowl, combine liquid egg product, cooled
cooked onion, ham, Molly McButter, corn, and salt and black
pepper. Mix thoroughly.

Spray medium skillet with nonstick cooking spray. Place
skillet over medium heat and add egg mixture. This is cooked

like an omelet. Using a spatula, lift the edges and let the liquid egg flow under; continue same procedure until all egg is becoming set. Place lid on skillet to finish cooking entire frittata, or if you wish you can turn it.

Serve warm with a few spoonfuls of marinara sauce on top as garnish, if desired.

Each serving provides:

111	Calories	.36 g	Fat
14.16 g	Protein	286 g	Sodium
13.02 g	Carbohydrate	2.08 mg	Cholesterol

Diabetic exchanges: Very lean meat, 2; starch, ½

3

Main Dishes

Spaghetti with Olives

SERVES 4

1 small onion, chopped
2 cloves garlic, pressed
¾ cup fresh sliced mushrooms
1 can (14½ ounces) tomato sauce
1½ cups fat-free chicken broth
¼ teaspoon dry oregano
   Salt and black pepper to taste
⅓ cup green salad olives, drained
3¾ cups cooked spaghetti

Spray medium saucepan with nonstick cooking spray. Add onion, garlic, and mushrooms. Cook and stir over medium-low heat 5 to 8 minutes. Add all remaining ingredients, except olives, and simmer over low heat 15 to 20 minutes. Stir in olives, just before serving. Serve over cooked spaghetti.

Each serving provides:

252	Calories	2.46 g	Fat
9.32 g	Protein	1370 g	Sodium
0 g	Carbohydrate	0 mg	Cholesterol

Diabetic exchanges: Very lean meat, 1; vegetable, 1; starch, 2½

Spinach Lasagna

SERVES 6

½ cup frozen chopped spinach, thawed and drained
1 cup 1 percent cottage cheese
1 small onion, chopped
1 clove garlic, pressed
¼ cup fat-free liquid egg product
1 can (10¾ ounces) Campbell's 98 percent fat-free cream of mushroom soup
¼ cup fat-free sour cream
2 teaspoons Molly McButter butter sprinkles
½ cup fat-free chicken broth
Salt and black pepper to taste
½ cup shredded fat-free mozzarella cheese
¼ cup fat-free Parmesan cheese
4 lasagna noodles, cooked

Preheat oven to 350 degrees.

In medium bowl, combine spinach, cottage cheese, onion, garlic, and liquid egg product.

In another bowl, combine soup, sour cream, and Molly McButter. Stir with spoon until smooth. Add chicken broth, salt and black pepper, and mix.

Spray glass loaf pan or medium glass baking dish with nonstick cooking spray. Beginning with spinach mixture, layer all ingredients in baking dish, including shredded mozzarella. Top with Parmesan cheese and bake at 350 degrees for about 1 hour.

Each serving provides:

182	Calories	2.02 g	Fat
13.81 g	Protein	795 g	Sodium
25.77 g	Carbohydrate	6.61 mg	Cholesterol

Diabetic exchanges: Very lean meat, 2; vegetable, 1; starch, 1

Creamy Mushroom Sauce over Tortellini

SERVES 3

½ small onion, chopped
½ cup fat-free chicken broth
⅓ cup fat-free cream cheese
½ cup 98 percent fat-free Campbell's cream of mushroom soup
1 teaspoon Molly McButter butter sprinkles
3 tablespoons shredded Parmesan cheese
⅛ teaspoon onion powder
Pinch of Italian seasoning
Garlic salt to taste
Black pepper to taste
2 cups cooked tortellini

Garnish
3 tablespoons fresh grated Parmesan cheese
1 tablespoon fresh parsley, chopped

Spray small skillet with nonstick cooking spray. Add onion and brown. Add chicken broth and simmer, covered, until onion is tender. Remove from heat and set aside.

In medium bowl, cream the cream cheese with electric mixer until smooth. Gradually add cream of mushroom soup and mix thoroughly.

Combine all ingredients, except tortellini, in medium saucepan. Stir and mix over low heat until heated through.

Serve over tortellini. Garnish with a sprinkle of fresh chopped parsley and grated Parmesan.

Each serving provides:

316	Calories	7.89 g	Fat
19.76 g	Protein	1636 g	Sodium
40.69 g	Carbohydrate	11.85 mg	Cholesterol

Diabetic exchanges: Lean meat, 2; starch, 2½

Shrimp Scampi over Pasta

 1 teaspoon olive oil
½ pound cooked and peeled medium shrimp
 3 cloves garlic, pressed
 1 cup fat-free chicken broth
 1 tablespoon fresh parsley, chopped
 1 teaspoon Molly McButter butter sprinkles
 2 tablespoons white cooking wine
     Black pepper to taste
1½ tablespoons cornstarch
1½ cups cooked pasta

Spray medium skillet with olive oil cooking spray. Add 1 teaspoon olive oil. Add shrimp and garlic and sauté over medium-low heat for 3 to 4 minutes.

Add chicken broth, parsley, Molly McButter, cooking wine, and black pepper to taste. Take a small amount of this broth mixture and add the cornstarch; stir until smooth, then add to the rest of the mixture in skillet. Simmer and stir until sauce slightly thickens.

Serve over cooked pasta.

Each serving provides:

333	Calories	4.31 g	Fat
30.14 g	Protein	934 g	Sodium
38.52 g	Carbohydrate	221 mg	Cholesterol

Diabetic exchanges: Very lean meat, 3; starch, 2¼; fat, 1

Pesto Chicken Pasta

SERVES 2

1 boneless, skinless chicken breast (4 ounces),
  cut in strips
¾ cup fat-free chicken broth
½ teaspoon Molly McButter butter sprinkles
½ small onion, chopped
1 clove garlic, pressed
  Salt and black pepper to taste
1 tablespoon pesto sauce (I bought the kind in a jar,
  but use fresh if you desire.)
1½ cups cooked angel hair pasta

Spray small skillet with nonstick cooking spray. Brown chicken strips over medium heat for about 10 minutes, then add a little water to the skillet, cover, and simmer until chicken is done. Set aside.

In small saucepan, combine chicken broth, Molly McButter, onion, and garlic. Simmer over low heat until onion is tender. Season with salt and black pepper. Remove from heat and stir in pesto. Pour over cooked pasta and toss. Top each serving with cooked chicken strips.

Each serving provides:

261	Calories	4.35	g	Fat
19.88 g	Protein	600	g	Sodium
34.42 g	Carbohydrate	32.67	mg	Cholesterol

Diabetic exchanges: Lean meat, 2; starch, 2

Ravioli with Butter Sauce and Cheese

1 cup refrigerated-type light cheese ravioli, cooked and drained
¼ cup water
1 tablespoon Molly McButter butter sprinkles
1 teaspoon lemon juice
⅛ teaspoon garlic powder
4 tablespoons fancy shredded Parmesan cheese

Spray medium saucepan with nonstick cooking spray. Place cooked and drained ravioli in saucepan. Add water, Molly McButter, lemon juice, and garlic powder. Simmer for 2 to 3 minutes, or until liquid cooks down a little. Stir frequently. Add Parmesan cheese, stir, and mix for 1 to 2 minutes. Serve warm.

Each serving provides:

181	Calories	4.50 g	Fat
10.20 g	Protein	627 g	Sodium
21.73 g	Carbohydrate	25.50 mg	Cholesterol

Diabetic exchanges: Medium meat, 1; starch, 1½

Prosciutto, Garlic, and Tomatoes over Noodles

SERVES 2

1 cup canned diced tomatoes
½ small onion, chopped
2 cloves garlic, pressed
⅓ cup fat-free chicken broth
½ teaspoon Italian seasoning
   Black pepper to taste
2 slices prosciutto
2 cups cooked "No Yolk" noodles

Combine tomatoes, onion, garlic, chicken broth, Italian seasoning, and black pepper in medium saucepan. Simmer and cook over low heat until onion is done (15 to 20 minutes).

   Add prosciutto and simmer about 2 more minutes. Serve over cooked noodles.

Each serving provides:

289	Calories	3.39 g	Fat
13.56 g	Protein	777 g	Sodium
50.20 g	Carbohydrate	12.50 mg	Cholesterol

Diabetic exchanges: Lean meat, 1; vegetable, 1; starch, 2½

Angel Hair Pasta with Cheese Sauce

1½ cups fat-free chicken broth
½ teaspoon Molly McButter butter sprinkles
2 pieces sun-dried tomatoes, cut into small pieces
   Dash of garlic salt
   Black pepper to taste
½ cup fat-free cream cheese
½ cup Kraft fat-free shredded mozzarella
¼ cup shredded Parmesan cheese
3 cups cooked angel hair pasta

Place first five ingredients in medium saucepan. Bring to a boil and reduce heat and simmer on low for 15 to 18 minutes. Stir occasionally.

In medium bowl, mix cream cheese with electric mixer until smooth. Add mozzarella and Parmesan and continue mixing. Use a whisk and add the cheese mixture to the chicken broth mixture. Turn heat off and continue to mix with whisk. Serve over angel hair pasta.

Each serving provides:

232	Calories	2.23 g	Fat
17.55 g	Protein	874 g	Sodium
33.97 g	Carbohydrate	9.14 mg	Cholesterol

Diabetic exchanges: Very lean meat, 2; starch, 2

Penne with Mushroom Garlic Cream Sauce

SERVES 4

    3 cloves garlic, pressed
    1 small onion, chopped
 1⅓ cups fat-free chicken broth
    1 teaspoon Molly McButter butter sprinkles
    2 cups fresh sliced mushrooms
       Salt and black pepper to taste
   ½ cup skim milk
   ½ cup fat-free sour cream
    1 tablespoon fresh basil, chopped
    3 cups cooked penne pasta

Spray medium saucepan with nonstick cooking spray. Add garlic and onion and cook over medium-low heat until onion becomes light brown. Add chicken broth, Molly McButter, mushrooms, and salt and black pepper to taste. Simmer over medium-low heat for about 8 minutes or until mushrooms are done. Add milk and whisk in sour cream. Simmer and stir for 2 to 3 minutes. Add basil and stir. Pour over penne pasta and serve.

Each serving provides:

210	Calories	.98 g	Fat
10.03 g	Protein	415 g	Sodium
40.22 g	Carbohydrate	.50 mg	Cholesterol

Diabetic exchanges: Vegetable, 1; starch, 2; skim milk, ¼

Pasta Shells
Filled with Cheese

SERVES 3

12 jumbo pasta shells, cooked according to
    package directions

Filling
½ cup 1 percent cottage cheese, drained
2 tablespoons roasted sweet pepper strips, diced
2 green onions, sliced
2 tablespoons fat-free liquid egg product
½ cup Kraft fat-free shredded mozzarella cheese
4 tablespoons shredded Parmesan cheese
   Garlic salt to taste
   Black pepper to taste

Topping
1 can (14½ ounces) chopped tomatoes
3 tablespoons shredded Parmesan cheese,
   as garnish for serving

Preheat oven to 350 degrees.

Cook pasta shells according to package directions, drain, and cool.

Combine all ingredients for filling in medium bowl and stir until mixed thoroughly. Spray 8 × 8-inch glass baking dish with nonstick cooking spray.

Begin filling each shell with cheese mixture and place in baking dish. You will need to fill 9 shells. I always cook a few extra shells in case one tears while filling. After all shells are filled, spread them out in the dish, so there is space between them.

Gently pour chopped tomatoes over all shells in the dish. Cover and bake for 45 minutes at 350 degrees. Garnish each serving with 1 tablespoon shredded Parmesan cheese, just before serving. Three shells equal 1 serving.

Each serving provides:

247	Calories	4.69 g	Fat
21.53 g	Protein	920 g	Sodium
29.82 g	Carbohydrate	14.33 mg	Cholesterol

Diabetic exchanges: Very lean meat, 2½; vegetable, 1½; starch, 1½

Pasta with Sweet Basil Cream Sauce

SERVES 2

½ cup fat-free cream cheese
½ cup fat-free chicken broth
½ teaspoon Molly McButter butter sprinkles
½ teaspoon dry onion flakes
⅛ teaspoon onion powder
Dash of garlic salt
Black pepper to taste
2 tablespoons fresh sweet basil, chopped
1½ cups cooked angel hair pasta
2 tablespoons fancy shredded Parmesan cheese, for garnish

Cream the cream cheese in a small bowl with electric mixer until smooth. Using a spoon, gradually stir in chicken broth. Stir in next 5 ingredients. Place mixture in small saucepan, simmer, and stir over low heat for about 10 minutes.

Remove from heat and stir in basil. Serve sauce over pasta. Garnish each serving with shredded Parmesan cheese.

Each serving provides:

238	Calories	2.21 g	Fat
17.75 g	Protein	813 g	Sodium
35.32 g	Carbohydrate	9.28 mg	Cholesterol

Diabetic exchanges: Very lean meat, 2; starch, 2

Pasta Primavera

2 cups cooked "No Yolk" extra wide noodles

½ cup sliced carrots
1 cup fresh sliced mushrooms
½ cup fresh snow peas
¾ cup fresh broccoli pieces
1 medium fresh tomato, cut into small chunks

Sauce
½ cup fat-free chicken broth
1 clove garlic, pressed
¼ cup skim milk
¼ cup evaporated skim milk
¼ cup fat-free sour cream
1 teaspoon Molly McButter butter sprinkles
3 tablespoons fat-free Parmesan cheese
   Salt and black pepper to taste
1 tablespoon all-purpose flour

Cook noodles according to package directions, drain, and cool.

Steam all vegetables, except tomato. Do not overcook. Set aside while making sauce.

In a medium saucepan, combine all ingredients for sauce, except flour. Stir over medium heat. Mix a small amount of the sauce liquid with the flour to make a thin paste. Stir until smooth. Pour flour mixture back into sauce and stir constantly over low heat, until sauce thickens. Sauce should turn out fairly thin and not thick.

Add fresh tomato chunks to vegetables and pour vegetables over bed of cooked noodles. Pour sauce over the top. Serve and enjoy.

Each serving provides:

191	Calories	.92 g	Fat
10.32 g	Protein	291 g	Sodium
34.99 g	Carbohydrate	3.38 mg	Cholesterol

Diabetic exchanges: Very lean meat, 1; vegetable, 1; starch, 1; skim milk, ½

Shrimp Scampi

¾ cup hot water
1 package (½ ounce) dry Butter Buds
1 tablespoon Molly McButter butter sprinkles
Juice from 1 fresh lemon
4 cloves garlic, pressed
8 large shrimp, peeled and deveined
½ teaspoon parsley flakes
1 green onion, sliced
Black pepper to taste
1½ cups cooked pasta (of your choice)

Spray large skillet with nonstick cooking spray.

In small bowl, combine water, Butter Buds, Molly McButter, lemon juice, and garlic. Place shrimp in skillet and pour butter mixture over shrimp. Cover and simmer over low heat for 7 to 9 minutes. Stir occasionally while cooking. Add parsley, green onion, and black pepper, and stir. Serve over your favorite pasta.

Each serving provides:

311	Calories	2.97 g	Fat
28.66 g	Protein	815 g	Sodium
42.31 g	Carbohydrate	172 mg	Cholesterol

Diabetic exchanges: Very lean meat, 3; starch, 2½

Angel Hair Pasta with Creamy Sausage Sauce

SERVES 2

1 link of sweet Italian turkey sausage, sliced
½ small onion, chopped
½ cup fat-free cream cheese
¾ cup fat-free chicken broth
⅛ teaspoon onion powder
⅛ teaspoon garlic powder
1 cup cooked angel hair pasta

Spray small skillet with nonstick cooking spray; brown and cook sliced sausage and onion until done. Set aside.

In small bowl, mix cream cheese with electric mixer until smooth. Gradually add chicken broth and mix as it is added. Add onion powder, garlic powder, and cooked sausage and onion. Pour into small saucepan and stir over medium-low heat for 4 to 5 minutes.

Serve over angel hair pasta.

Each serving provides:

239	Calories	3.52 g	Fat
21.57 g	Protein	1173 g	Sodium
27.48 g	Carbohydrate	30.28 mg	Cholesterol

Diabetic exchanges: Very lean meat, 3; vegetable, 1; starch, 1¼

Mushroom Pie Deluxe

SERVES 8

8   cups fresh sliced mushrooms
1   medium onion, chopped
2   cloves garlic, pressed
1   regular-sized frozen Pet Ritz piecrust
1   can (10¾ ounces) Campbell's 98 percent fat-free
    cream of mushroom soup
½   cup fat-free sour cream
1   egg white
1   tablespoon Molly McButter butter sprinkles
    Dash of dry oregano leaves
    Salt to taste
    Plenty of black pepper
1   cup Kraft shredded fat-free mozzarella
½   cup shredded Parmesan cheese

Preheat oven to 350 degrees.

Spray large cooking pot with nonstick cooking spray. Add mushrooms, onion, and garlic. Stir over medium heat until mushrooms are done and all the liquid has cooked away. Set aside to cool slightly.

Spray glass pie plate with nonstick cooking spray. Transfer frozen piecrust from aluminum pie plate to glass plate. This works best if the piecrust is frozen. It will usually pop out of the aluminum plate easily. Let frozen crust thaw after transferring and then form and press into glass plate. Set aside.

In medium bowl, combine mushroom soup, sour cream, egg white, and Molly McButter. Mix with electric mixer until well blended. Pour this mixture over mushrooms and add oregano, salt, and black pepper.

Spoon about a third of the mushroom mixture into piecrust. Sprinkle on half of the shredded mozzarella cheese. Add another third of the mushroom mixture and sprinkle on the remaining shredded mozzarella. Top with all the rest of the mushroom mixture. Sprinkle the top with half of the shredded Parmesan cheese. Reserve the other half for garnish, just before serving.

Bake at 350 degrees for 50 to 55 minutes.

Each serving provides:

186	Calories	6.80 g	Fat
11.06 g	Protein	608 g	Sodium
19.59 g	Carbohydrate	10.45 mg	Cholesterol

Diabetic exchanges: Very lean meat, 1; lean meat, 1; starch, 1; skim milk, ¼

Meatballs with Mushroom Sauce

SERVES 5

Meatballs
½ pound ground turkey breast
⅓ cup cracker crumbs
1 tablespoon dry onion flakes
3 tablespoons fat-free liquid egg product
⅛ teaspoon oregano leaves
    Salt and black pepper to taste

Sauce
1 can (10¾ ounces) Campbell's 98 percent fat-free
   cream of mushroom soup
1 cup skim milk
¼ cup fat-free sour cream

4½ cups pasta, noodles, or rice

Combine all ingredients for meatballs in medium bowl and mix. Form into walnut-sized balls. Spray large skillet with nonstick cooking spray, and brown and cook meatballs. Set aside when done.

In medium bowl, combine ingredients for sauce. Use a whisk and blend ingredients until smooth. Pour sauce over meatballs and simmer for 10 to 15 minutes. Serve over pasta, noodles, or rice.

Each serving provides:

154	Calories	3.22 g	Fat
15.37 g	Protein	598 g	Sodium
14.63 g	Carbohydrate	29.54 mg	Cholesterol

Diabetic exchanges: Very lean meat, 1; lean meat, 1; starch, ½; skim milk, ¼

Meat and Cheese Ravioli

SERVES 3

Filling
½ pound ground turkey breast
½ cup lowfat shredded mozzarella cheese
3 green onions, chopped
⅛ teaspoon Italian seasoning
⅛ teaspoon fennel
   Salt and black pepper to taste

Dough
1 cup all-purpose flour
1 egg white, slightly beaten
⅓ cup water
½ teaspoon salt

1 cup lowfat pasta sauce.
2 tablespoons fat-free Parmesan cheese
1 tablespoon fresh parsley, chopped

In medium bowl, combine all ingredients for filling. Mix and set aside.

Combine ingredients for dough in medium bowl and mix. Place dough on floured surface and kneed for 5 to 6 minutes. Using a rolling pin, roll dough out on floured surface to about one-quarter-inch thick. If you have a ravioli maker, they work great. If not, cut small round discs with a small glass or small biscuit cutter.

Using a medium pot, fill it half full of water and start to boil on stove.

Place a small ball of meat and cheese mixture in the center of circle of cut-out dough. Fold half of circle over meat and cheese ball to form a sort of half moon. Pinch all edges firmly to seal. Repeat until all dough or meat mixture is gone.

Drop each filled ravioli into boiling water. You can usually put several in the pot to cook at one time. Reduce heat and cook gently for about 10 minutes.

Use a slotted spoon to lift cooked ravioli from water. Place all ravioli in serving dish and pour pasta sauce over the top and serve. Garnish with Parmesan cheese and parsley.

	Each serving provides:		
336	Calories	3.65 g	Fat
32.21 g	Protein	759 g	Sodium
41.92 g	Carbohydrate	52.03 mg	Cholesterol
	Diabetic exchanges: Very lean meat, 5; starch, 2		

Meat and Mushroom Calzone

¼ pound extra-lean ground beef
1 cup fresh sliced mushrooms
1 small onion, chopped
2 cloves fresh garlic, pressed
⅓ cup lowfat pasta sauce
  Salt and black pepper to taste
½ roll refrigerated pizza dough
4 tablespoons fat-free mozzarella cheese
4 tablespoons fat-free Parmesan cheese

Preheat oven to 375 degrees.

Spray medium skillet with nonstick cooking spray. Add ground beef and brown over medium heat. Add mushrooms, onion, and garlic, and continue to cook and brown for 4 to 6 minutes. Add pasta sauce and salt and black pepper to taste. Continue to stir over medium heat until mushrooms and onions are done. Remove from heat and set aside.

Spray baking sheet with nonstick cooking spray.

Cut pizza dough into two equal pieces. Spread and roll each piece of dough out to accommodate half of the meat mixture. Sprinkle each with 2 tablespoons of the Parmesan cheese and 2 tablespoons of the mozzarella cheese. Fold the dough over to make a sort of half moon and seal edges with your fingers or fork. Cut a small slit in the top of each one for venting steam.

Place on baking sheet and bake at 375 degrees for 25 to 30 minutes.

Each serving provides:

401	Calories	9.48 g	Fat
25.48 g	Protein	731 g	Sodium
49.28 g	Carbohydrate	43.63 mg	Cholesterol

Diabetic exchanges: Lean meat, 3; vegetable, 2; starch, 2¼

Spaghetti and Meatballs

SERVES 3

1½ cups cooked spaghetti

Meatballs
- ¼ pound extra-lean ground beef
- 2 tablespoons old-fashioned Quaker oats
- 2 teaspoons dry onion flakes
- ⅛ teaspoon black pepper
- 2½ tablespoons fat-free liquid egg product
- 1 clove garlic, pressed
- 2 tablespoons fat-free Parmesan cheese

Sauce
- 1½ cups tomato sauce
- 2 cloves garlic, pressed
- 1 medium onion, chopped
- ¼ teaspoon Italian seasoning
- ¼ teaspoon onion powder
- 2 tablespoons red cooking wine
- ½ cup canned sliced mushrooms

Cook spaghetti according to package directions, drain, and cool.

In medium bowl, mix together ingredients for meatballs. Form into balls. Spray medium skillet with nonstick cooking spray and brown meatballs on all sides. Set aside while preparing sauce.

In medium saucepan, combine all ingredients for sauce; stir and simmer over medium heat for 2 to 3 minutes. Add meatballs and simmer, covered, for 10 to 12 minutes.

Serve over cooked spaghetti.

Each serving provides:

299	Calories	7.51 g	Fat
15.90 g	Protein	1092 g	Sodium
41.01 g	Carbohydrate	28.0 mg	Cholesterol

Diabetic exchanges: Lean meat, 2; vegetable, 3; starch, 1¼

Linguine with Walnut and Basil Cream

SERVES 4

2 teaspoons walnut pieces
1 cup fat-free chicken broth
2 teaspoons dry onion flakes
 Salt and black pepper to taste
1 cup skim milk
½ teaspoon Molly McButter butter sprinkles
2 tablespoons fresh basil, chopped
½ cup fat-free sour cream
3 cups cooked linguine
4 tablespoons shredded Parmesan cheese, for garnish

Crush walnut pieces to bring out the flavor and set aside.

Using a medium saucepan, combine chicken broth, dry onion flakes, and salt and black pepper to taste. Stir over medium heat for 3 to 4 minutes. Reduce heat and add milk and Molly McButter. Simmer 2 to 3 minutes. Then add walnuts and basil and stir. Whisk in sour cream and serve over linguine. Garnish with shredded Parmesan cheese. Serve and enjoy.

Each serving provides:

229	Calories	3.05 g	Fat
11.99 g	Protein	522 g	Sodium
37.57 g	Carbohydrate	5.0 mg	Cholesterol

Diabetic exchanges: Very lean meat, ¾; starch, 2; skim milk, ½

Italian Vegetable and Meat Pie

SERVES 8

1 regular-sized Pet Ritz frozen piecrust
1 small onion, chopped
2 cups fresh mushrooms, sliced
1 cup zucchini, peeled and cubed
1 cup carrots, sliced
1 cup 1 percent cottage cheese
⅛ teaspoon dry oregano leaves
4 slices roasted bell pepper, cut into pieces
 Dash of crushed red pepper flakes
1 teaspoon Molly McButter butter sprinkles
1 cup Kraft fat-free shredded mozzarella cheese
 Salt and black pepper to taste
1 clove garlic, pressed
1 link sweet Italian turkey sausage, cut into small pieces
10 pieces turkey pepperoni, cut in small pieces
½ cup fat-free sour cream, for garnish

Preheat oven to 375 degrees.

Spray 9-inch glass pie plate with nonstick cooking spray. While piecrust is still frozen, gently remove it from the aluminum pie tin and place it in the glass pie plate. Let it thaw before pressing it into the shape of the glass plate.

Spray skillet with nonstick cooking spray. Add onion, mushrooms, zucchini, and carrots. Cook and stir over medium-low heat until carrots are starting to get tender (about 10 to 15 minutes).

Set aside.

In medium bowl, combine cottage cheese, oregano, roasted bell pepper, red pepper flakes, Molly McButter, shredded mozzarella cheese, salt and black pepper, and pressed garlic.

Spray small skillet with nonstick cooking spray and brown pieces of sweet Italian sausage (about 5 to 10 minutes). Reserve pepperoni and Italian sausage for top of pie.

Place vegetable mixture in unbaked piecrust. Spoon cottage cheese mixture on top of vegetables. Arrange pepperoni and Italian sausage on top of pie. Bake at 375 degrees for 30 to 35 minutes. Add a small spoonful of sour cream on top of each piece when serving.

Each serving provides:

175	Calories	5.49 g	Fat
13.37 g	Protein	479 g	Sodium
16.43 g	Carbohydrate	15.94 mg	Cholesterol

Diabetic exchanges: Very lean meat, 2; vegetable, 1; starch, 1

Angel Hair Pasta with Bacon and Sour Cream Sauce

SERVES 2

1¼ cups fat-free chicken broth
1 teaspoon Molly McButter butter sprinkles
1 green onion, sliced
Dash of garlic salt
Black pepper to taste
½ cup fat-free sour cream
4 slices crisp cooked turkey bacon, crumbled
1½ cups cooked angel hair pasta
4 tablespoons shredded Parmesan cheese, for garnish

MAIN DISHES
138

In medium saucepan, combine chicken broth, Molly Mc-Butter, and green onions. Simmer over low heat for 3 minutes. Add garlic salt and black pepper. Simmer another 3 minutes. Remove from heat, whisk in sour cream, add crumbled bacon. Serve over angel hair pasta and garnish with shredded Parmesan.

Each serving provides:

297	Calories	6.57 g	Fat
19.40 g	Protein	1422 g	Sodium
38.84 g	Carbohydrate	28.0 mg	Cholesterol

Diabetic exchanges: Lean meat, 2; starch, 2; skim milk, ⅓

Lasagna

4 lasagna noodles, cooked and drained
1 small onion, chopped
¼ red bell pepper, chopped
1 cup fresh sliced mushrooms
½ cup sliced zucchini
½ cup sliced carrots
1 clove garlic, pressed
1 cup lowfat spaghetti sauce
¼ teaspoon Italian seasoning
¼ teaspoon seasoned salt (optional)
¼ cup fat-free liquid egg product
1½ cups 1 percent cottage cheese
¾ cup Kraft fat-free shredded mozzarella cheese
4 tablespoons shredded Parmesan cheese
3 tablespoons fat-free Parmesan cheese

Preheat oven to 350 degrees.

Prepare noodles according to package directions.
   Spray large skillet with nonstick cooking spray. Add all vegetables and garlic, then simmer and cook until slightly tender, about 8 to 10 minutes.

In medium bowl, combine spaghetti sauce and spices. In another bowl, combine liquid egg product and cottage cheese.

Spray a glass loaf pan with nonstick cooking spray. Layer ingredients in pan, starting with part of the spaghetti sauce, then 2 lasagna noodles, half the vegetables, half the cottage cheese mixture, and half of each of the cheeses. Repeat layers until all ingredients are used. Cover and bake at 350 degrees for 1 hour.

Let stand about 10 to 15 minutes before serving.

Each serving provides:

297	Calories	3.02	g	Fat
27.40	g	Protein	864	g	Sodium
38.65	g	Carbohydrate	13.75	mg	Cholesterol

Diabetic exchanges: Very lean meat, 4; vegetable, 2; starch, 1¼

Italian Cheese Pie

SERVES 8

 1 regular-sized frozen Pet Ritz piecrust
1½ cups 1 percent cottage cheese, drained
 ¼ cup fat-free Parmesan cheese
10 pieces turkey pepperoni, cut into pieces
 ½ cup Healthy Choice lowfat, grated mozzarella cheese
 ¼ cup onion, finely chopped
 1 small tomato, chopped
 ¼ teaspoon garlic powder
 2 tablespoons green pepper, finely chopped
 ⅓ cup fat-free liquid egg product
   Black pepper to taste

Preheat oven to 350 degrees.

Spray 9-inch glass pie plate with nonstick cooking spray. Remove frozen piecrust from freezer and immediately pop it out of the aluminum pie plate. Place frozen crust into glass pie plate and set aside. Do not try to mash it into place.

In medium bowl, combine cottage cheese, Parmesan cheese, turkey pepperoni, grated mozzarella, onion, tomato, garlic powder, green pepper, egg product, and black pepper. Mix thoroughly with spoon.

Now gently form the thawed piecrust to the pie plate. If it is not quite thawed, place it in the microwave for about 15 seconds.

Pour cheese mixture into unbaked piecrust and bake at 350 degrees for 30 to 35 minutes. This is wonderful served with a crisp green salad.

Each serving provides:

151	Calories	5.15 g	Fat
10.60 g	Protein	383 g	Sodium
13.28 g	Carbohydrate	10.07 mg	Cholesterol

Diabetic exchanges: Lean meat, 1; vegetable, ½; starch, 1

Garlic Supreme Meatloaf

½ pound extra-lean ground beef
1 can (6 ounces) tomato paste
3 tablespoons fat-free liquid egg product
8 cloves garlic, pressed
1 teaspoon dry onion flakes
1 small onion, chopped
½ teaspoon dry celery flakes
⅛ teaspoon dry oregano flakes
2 slices sweet bell pepper, finely chopped
  Salt and black pepper to taste

Preheat oven to 350 degrees.

Use a large bowl and combine all ingredients, except half of the tomato paste. Mix thoroughly. Spray medium baking dish or pan with nonstick cooking spray. Form meatloaf mixture into an evenly shaped mound and place in baking dish. Top loaf with remaining tomato paste and bake at 350 degrees for 45 to 55 minutes. Serve with small baked potato if desired.

Each serving provides:

198	Calories	10.18 g	Fat
14.19 g	Protein	395 g	Sodium
13.54 g	Carbohydrate	39.0 mg	Cholesterol

Diabetic exchanges: Lean meat, 2; vegetable, 3

Ravioli and Cheese

1 cup 1 percent cottage cheese
2 teaspoons dry onion flakes
1 clove garlic, pressed
1 egg white, slightly beaten
½ cup Kraft fat-free mozzarella cheese
½ cup lowfat spaghetti sauce
   Black pepper to taste
2 cups refrigerated-type cheese ravioli, cooked according
   to package directions and drained

Preheat oven to 350 degrees.

In medium bowl, combine cottage cheese, onion flakes, garlic, egg white, and mozzarella cheese. Stir together with a spoon until thoroughly mixed.

Spray a medium-small baking dish with nonstick cooking spray. (I use a glass loaf pan.) Pour spaghetti sauce over bottom of dish. Add ravioli for the next layer. Top with cottage cheese mixture. Sprinkle on a little black pepper, if desired.

Place in oven at 350 degrees for 35 minutes.

Each serving provides:

202	Calories	2.88 g	Fat
20.58 g	Protein	744 g	Sodium
23.67 g	Carbohydrate	5.0 mg	Cholesterol

Diabetic exchanges: Very lean meat, 2; vegetable, 1; starch, 1¼

Seafood Stuffed Shells with Cream Sauce

SERVES 5

12 jumbo pasta shells (You will use only 10 pasta shells;
   the extras are in case one or two split.)

Stuffing
¼ pound ready-to-eat small shrimp
¼ pound ready-to-eat crab meat or imitation crab meat
½ cup soft bread crumbs
¼ cup onion, finely chopped
1 tablespoon fresh parsley, chopped
¼ cup fat-free liquid egg product
   Salt and black pepper to taste

Sauce
2 tablespoons fresh onion, minced
1 clove garlic, pressed
2 tablespoons white cooking wine
¼ cup skim milk
2 tablespoons flour
1 cup fat-free chicken broth
½ teaspoon Molly McButter butter sprinkles

Topping
¼ cup shredded Parmesan cheese

Preheat oven to 350 degrees.

Cook pasta shells according to package directions, drain, and cool.

Chop crab, shrimp, and bread crumbs in food processor. Spray skillet with nonstick cooking spray and sauté onion for about 3 minutes. Mix all remaining ingredients for stuffing together in a medium bowl.

Spray 8-inch glass baking dish with nonstick cooking spray. Stuff shells and place in baking dish.

Spray medium saucepan with nonstick cooking spray. Sauté onion and garlic for 1 to 2 minutes. Add wine and simmer 2 to 3 minutes. Mix milk and flour to make a smooth paste. Gradually add paste to chicken broth. Add Molly Mc-Butter and stir into onions and garlic in saucepan. Stir and cook until thickened.

Gently pour sauce over stuffed shells and top with shredded Parmesan cheese. Bake at 350 degrees for 20 minutes. Two shells equal one serving.

Each serving provides:

182	Calories	2.39 g	Fat
16.34 g	Protein	493 g	Sodium
21.57 g	Carbohydrate	70.42 mg	Cholesterol

Diabetic exchanges: Very lean meat, 2; vegetable, 1; starch, 1

Garlic Italian Chicken

2 boneless, skinless chicken breasts (3 ounces each)
2 tablespoons all-purpose flour
  Salt and black pepper to taste
½ teaspoon dried parsley flakes
4 cloves garlic, pressed
⅓ cup fat-free chicken broth
¾ cup lowfat pasta sauce
1½ cups cooked pasta (optional)

Sprinkle each side of chicken breasts lightly with flour. Season each side with salt, black pepper, and parsley. Spray small skillet with nonstick cooking spray. Brown chicken on both sides.

In small bowl, add pressed garlic and chicken broth to pasta sauce, and mix. Pour this mixture over chicken breasts and simmer over low heat for 10 to 15 minutes.

Serve chicken breasts over cooked pasta, if desired.

Each serving provides:

109	Calories	.47 g	Fat
9.63 g	Protein	479 g	Sodium
16.71 g	Carbohydrate	16.34 mg	Cholesterol

Diabetic exchanges: Very lean meat, 1; vegetable, 1½; starch, ½

Sweet Italian Sausage and Eggs

1 link sweet Italian turkey sausage, cut into small pieces
2 green onions, sliced
1 tablespoon green bell pepper, finely chopped
1 cup fat-free liquid egg product
⅓ cup Kraft fat-free shredded mozzarella cheese
  Salt and black pepper to taste
4 tablespoons shredded Parmesan cheese, for garnish

Spray medium skillet with nonstick cooking spray. Add sausage pieces, onion, and green pepper. Stir over medium heat until everything is cooked thoroughly.

In small bowl, combine egg product and mozzarella cheese. Stir with spoon until well blended. Add this mixture to skillet, and add salt and black pepper to taste. Do not stir in skillet. Cover skillet with lid and cook over low heat until egg is set. Garnish with shredded Parmesan cheese when done.

Each serving provides:

196	Calories	6.02 g	Fat
29.30 g	Protein	930 g	Sodium
3.79 g	Carbohydrate	36.33 mg	Cholesterol

Diabetic exchanges: Very lean meat, 4; vegetable, 1; starch, ¼

Garlic and Parmesan Chicken with Pasta

SERVES 2

 2 boneless, skinless chicken breasts (3 ounces each)
¼ teaspoon garlic powder
 1 teaspoon Molly McButter butter sprinkles
⅓ cup fat-free Parmesan cheese
 Black pepper to taste
¾ cup Barilla Mushroom and Garlic pasta sauce
⅓ cup fat-free chicken broth
1½ cups cooked pasta

Sprinkle each side of chicken breasts with garlic powder, Molly McButter, and fat-free Parmesan cheese. Add black pepper to taste.

Spray medium skillet with nonstick cooking spray. Brown chicken breasts on both sides over low heat.

In small bowl, combine pasta sauce and chicken broth, and mix with spoon. Pour this mixture around chicken breasts in skillet. Cover and simmer over low heat for 10 to 15 minutes.

Serve chicken over cooked pasta.

Each serving provides:

358	Calories	3.26 g	Fat
29.40 g	Protein	1046 g	Sodium
47.90 g	Carbohydrate	57.01 mg	Cholesterol

Diabetic exchanges: Very lean meat, 4; vegetable, 2; starch, 2

Fettucine Alfredo

½ cup fat-free cream cheese
½ cup fat-free chicken broth
⅛ teaspoon garlic salt
⅛ teaspoon onion powder
2 tablespoons shredded Parmesan cheese
½ teaspoon lemon juice
½ teaspoon Molly McButter butter sprinkles
⅛ teaspoon black pepper
Dash of seasoned salt (optional)
1½ cups cooked fettucine

In small bowl, mix cream cheese with electric mixer until smooth. Gradually add chicken broth and stir with spoon until well blended. Add all remaining ingredients, except fettucine. Pour sauce mixture into small saucepan. Cook and stir over medium heat until mixture comes to a boil. Reduce heat and continue stirring for 4 to 5 minutes.

Serve sauce over fettucine.

Each serving provides:

236	Calories	2.20 g	Fat
17.67 g	Protein	934 g	Sodium
35.09 g	Carbohydrate	9.28 mg	Cholesterol

Diabetic exchanges: Lean meat, 2; starch, 2

Italian Meatloaf

2 pounds fresh ground turkey breast
⅓ cup fat-free liquid egg product
½ cup tomato sauce
2 tablespoons dry onion flakes
½ teaspoon garlic powder
1 tablespoon dry green pepper flakes
1 teaspoon Worcestershire sauce
½ teaspoon Italian seasoning
½ cup fat-free Parmesan cheese
½ cup Kraft fat-free shredded mozzarella cheese

Preheat oven to 350 degrees.

In large bowl, combine all ingredients and stir with large spoon until thoroughly mixed. Spray large loaf pan with non-stick cooking spray. Pour meatloaf mixture into loaf pan and bake at 350 degrees for 1 hour. Great with a baked potato or sliced cold on a sandwich.

Each serving provides:

110	Calories	1.20 g	Fat
20.56 g	Protein	181 g	Sodium
2.90 g	Carbohydrate	47.19 mg	Cholesterol

Diabetic exchanges: Very lean meat, 3

Elegant Chicken Pasta

2   cloves garlic, pressed
2   boneless, skinless chicken breasts (3 ounces each),
    cut into small pieces
1   cup tomatoes, peeled and chopped
1   cup canned artichoke hearts, chopped
¾   cup white cooking wine
½   cup fat-free chicken broth
2   tablespoons fresh chopped basil
3   cups cooked pasta (of your choice)
¼   cup shredded Parmesan cheese

Spray skillet with olive oil spray. Over medium heat, stir garlic about 1 minute, then add chicken pieces. Stir and cook until chicken is done, about 10 to 15 minutes. Add 1 to 2 tablespoons chicken broth if skillet becomes too dry.

Add tomatoes, artichoke hearts, white wine, and broth to chicken in skillet. Stir and simmer over low-medium heat for 10 minutes. Remove from heat and stir in fresh basil. Serve over your favorite cooked pasta. Top with a sprinkling of shredded Parmesan cheese.

Each serving provides:

276	Calories	3.0 g	Fat
18.69 g	Protein	745 g	Sodium
36.18 g	Carbohydrate	28.51 mg	Cholesterol

Diabetic exchanges: Very lean meat, 2; vegetable, 2; starch, 2

Eggplant and Mushroom Casserole

SERVES 6

1½ cups eggplant, peeled and cut into small cubes
  1 medium onion, chopped
  2 cups fresh sliced mushrooms
  1 clove garlic, pressed
  1 cup carrots, sliced
  2 small strips roasted bell pepper, cut into small pieces
 ¼ cup fat-free chicken broth
  1 cup frozen corn
  1 cup Kraft shredded fat-free mozzarella
    Garlic salt to taste
    Black pepper to taste

Topping
½ cup crushed corn flakes
½ teaspoon Molly McButter butter sprinkles

Preheat oven to 350 degrees.

Spray large skillet with nonstick cooking spray. Add eggplant, onion, mushrooms, and garlic, and simmer over medium-low heat. Add carrots and roasted bell pepper, and continue to simmer for about 15 minutes. Add chicken broth and corn, and simmer for 5 more minutes. Season with garlic salt and black pepper.

Spray medium baking dish with nonstick cooking spray. (I used a glass loaf pan.) In small bowl, combine corn flakes and Molly McButter, and stir until thoroughly mixed. Pour a small amount of eggplant mixture in bottom of baking dish, then add a layer of shredded cheese. Repeat this process until all is used. Sprinkle corn flake topping evenly over the top and bake at 350 degrees for 30 minutes.

Each serving provides:

111	Calories	.48 g	Fat
8.56 g	Protein	282 g	Sodium
19.51 g	Carbohydrate	3.33 mg	Cholesterol

Diabetic exchanges: Very lean meat, 1; vegetable, 1½; starch, ½

Italian Chicken and Vegetable Pie

1   cup carrots, sliced
1   cup fresh mushrooms, sliced
1   small onion, chopped
1   raw boneless, skinless chicken breast (4 ounces),
     cut into small pieces
1   can (10¾ ounces) 98 percent fat-free
     cream of mushroom soup
½   cup fat-free sour cream
1   tablespoon Molly McButter butter sprinkles
1   cup fat-free chicken broth
2   teaspoons dry onion flakes
     Pinch of dry oregano flakes
     Salt and black pepper to taste
¾   cup water
1   cup lowfat or light pancake mix (dry)
¼   cup shredded Parmesan cheese

Preheat oven to 350 degrees.

Spray medium saucepan with nonstick cooking spray. Add carrots, mushrooms, and onion. Stir and cook over medium heat for 8 to 10 minutes. Add chicken pieces and continue cooking until chicken is browned.

In medium bowl, combine cream of mushroom soup, sour cream, Molly McButter, chicken broth, dry onion flakes, dry oregano, and salt and black pepper to taste.

In another medium bowl, combine water and pancake mix and stir. Spray 11 × 7-inch glass baking dish with nonstick cooking spray. Pour about a third of the pancake mix in the bottom of the baking dish.

Combine soup mixture with chicken and vegetables and stir. Pour this mixture into the baking dish with the pancake mixture, which has already been poured. Distribute the filling evenly over bottom, then gently pour the remaining pancake mixture over the top and cover as much of the top as evenly as possible. Sprinkle on Parmesan cheese.

Bake at 350 degrees for 40 to 45 minutes.

Each serving provides:

135	Calories	2.92	g	Fat
7.61	g Protein	700	g	Sodium
19.32	g Carbohydrate	11.12	mg	Cholesterol

Diabetic exchanges: Lean meat, 1; starch, 1

Shrimp and Crab Stuffed Shells

SERVES 4

12 jumbo pasta shells

Filling
¼ pound ready-to-eat small shrimp, cut into small pieces
¼ pound ready-to-eat flaked crab or imitation crab meat
½ small onion, finely chopped
1 clove garlic, pressed
1 teaspoon lemon juice
½ teaspoon Molly McButter butter sprinkles
¼ cup Kraft shredded fat-free mozzarella cheese
   Salt and black pepper to taste

Sauce
1 cup fat-free chicken broth
2 teaspoons dry onion flakes
2 tablespoons white cooking wine
1 cup skim milk
½ teaspoon Molly McButter butter sprinkles
½ cup fat-free sour cream

½ cup shredded Parmesan cheese, for topping

Preheat oven to 350 degrees.

Cook pasta shells according to package directions, drain, and cool.

Arrange shells in 9-inch square glass baking dish, sprayed with nonstick cooking spray. In medium bowl, combine ingredients for filling. Mix thoroughly. Fill shells with mixture.

In medium saucepan, combine ingredients for sauce, except sour cream. Cook over low heat for 3 to 4 minutes. Whisk in sour cream and gently pour over stuffed shells. Sprinkle top with Parmesan cheese. Bake at 350 degrees for 30 to 35 minutes. One serving equals three shells.

Each serving provides:

279	Calories	4.40 g	Fat
26.60 g	Protein	770 g	Sodium
30.92 g	Carbohydrate	93.95 mg	Cholesterol

Diabetic exchanges: Very lean meat, 4; starch, 1¼; skim milk, ¼

Creamy Mushroom Lasagna

- 4 lasagna noodles
- 4 cups mushrooms, sliced
- 1 cup 1 percent cottage cheese
- ¼ cup fat-free liquid egg product
- 1 clove garlic, pressed
- ½ cup Kraft fat-free mozzarella cheese
  Salt and black pepper to taste
- 1 can (10¾ ounces) Campbell's 98 percent fat-free
  cream of mushroom soup
- ½ cup canned evaporated skim milk
- ¾ cup fat-free sour cream
- 1 tablespoon Molly McButter butter sprinkles
- 1 teaspoon dry onion flakes

Preheat oven to 350 degrees.

Cook lasagna noodles according to package directions, drain, and cool.

Cook sliced mushrooms in a medium pan. When tender, pour off any extra liquid and set aside.

In medium bowl, combine cottage cheese, egg product, garlic, mozzarella, and salt and black pepper. Stir and mix with spoon.

In another medium bowl, combine soup, skim milk, sour cream, Molly McButter, and onion flakes. Mix with electric mixer or whisk until smooth.

Spray glass loaf pan with nonstick cooking spray. Starting with half the soup mixture on the bottom, add 2 lasagna noodles, half the mushrooms, then half the cottage cheese mixture. Repeat layers for remaining ingredients. Bake at 350 degrees for 45 minutes to 1 hour. Let stand about 15 minutes after removing from oven before serving.

Each serving provides:

298	Calories	3.30 g	Fat
24.23 g	Protein	1087 g	Sodium
42.02 g	Carbohydrate	8.15 mg	Cholesterol

Diabetic exchanges: Very lean meat, 3; starch, 1¼; skim milk, 1

Chicken and Spaghetti Casserole

Serves 6

2 tablespoons chopped almonds, toasted
3 tablespoons all-purpose flour
¾ cup canned evaporated fat-free milk
½ cup fat-free chicken broth
1 tablespoon Molly McButter butter sprinkles
   Garlic salt to taste
   Black pepper to taste
¾ cup cooked, chopped chicken breast
4½ cups cooked spaghetti (Cook spaghetti in a
   couple of cans of fat-free chicken broth and
   then add water to a suitable level.)
½ cup fat-free shredded Cheddar cheese

Preheat oven to 350 degrees.

Toast chopped almonds by placing them in a small pan in the oven at 350 degrees, 5 to 8 minutes. Once the almonds start to brown, remove from oven. These burn very quickly after browning begins.

Make white sauce by stirring flour in skillet over medium heat until flour is starting to brown. Slowly add milk and chicken broth, stirring with whisk to make a smooth mixture. When mixture thickens, remove from heat and stir in Molly McButter, garlic salt, and black pepper. Stir in chicken and cooked spaghetti. Spread evenly in an 8 × 8-inch glass baking dish that has been sprayed with nonstick cooking spray.

Sprinkle chopped almonds over top, then cover with Cheddar cheese for topping. Bake at 350 degrees for 15 minutes.

Each serving provides:

253	Calories	2.97 g	Fat
16.93 g	Protein	438 g	Sodium
38.55 g	Carbohydrate	16.42 mg	Cholesterol

Diabetic exchanges: Very lean meat, 2; starch, 2; fat, ½

Chicken Marsala

4 boneless, skinless chicken breasts (3 ounces each)
   Garlic powder
   Black pepper

Sauce
¼ cup marsala cooking wine
   (available at most supermarkets)
1½ cups fat-free chicken broth
1½ tablespoons Molly McButter butter sprinkles
1 teaspoon dry onion flakes
1 clove garlic, pressed
¼ cup evaporated skim milk
1 cup fresh sliced mushrooms
   Black pepper to taste
1 tablespoon cornstarch
¼ cup cold water

Spray large skillet with nonstick cooking spray. Season each side of chicken breasts with garlic powder and black pepper. Place in skillet and brown; continue cooking over low heat until done. Remove chicken from skillet and set aside.

Pour cooking wine into skillet and stir over low heat for 1 minute. Add chicken broth, Molly McButter, onion flakes, and garlic, and stir 1 minute. Add evaporated milk and mushrooms, then simmer and stir until mushrooms are tender, 2 to 3 minutes. Add black pepper.

In small bowl, mix cornstarch and water with spoon until smooth. Add this mixture to skillet and stir until sauce thickens. Remove from heat and add chicken breasts back to skillet.

Serve over angel hair pasta, if desired.

Each serving provides:

146	Calories	1.16 g	Fat
22.12 g	Protein	740 g	Sodium
9.01 g	Carbohydrate	49.64 mg	Cholesterol

Diabetic exchanges: Very lean meat, 5; skim milk, ½

Eggplant Casserole

1 small eggplant, peeled and diced
1 teaspoon salt
2½ cups dry stuffing mix
1 small onion, chopped
½ cup fat-free Parmesan cheese
1 teaspoon Molly McButter butter sprinkles
½ cup fat-free chicken broth
½ cup fat-free liquid egg product
   Salt and black pepper to taste

Preheat oven to 350 degrees.

In medium saucepan, cover eggplant with water, add 1 teaspoon salt, and cook over medium heat until eggplant is tender. Drain and set aside to cool.

Combine eggplant with all remaining ingredients and mix. Spray medium baking dish with nonstick cooking spray. Pour in eggplant mixture and bake at 350 degrees for 40 to 45 minutes.

Each serving provides:

96	Calories	.19 g	Fat
4.70 g	Protein	544 g	Sodium
18.91 g	Carbohydrate	2.0 mg	Cholesterol

Diabetic exchanges: Vegetable, 2; starch, ½

Chicken Mozzarella

2 boneless, skinless chicken breasts (3 ounces each)
1 egg white, slightly beaten
½ cup crushed corn flakes
2 tablespoons water
1 cup lowfat spaghetti sauce
½ cup Kraft fat-free shredded mozzarella cheese

Preheat oven to 350 degrees.

Spray small skillet with nonstick cooking spray. Dip chicken breasts in egg white and roll in corn flakes. Place in skillet and brown on each side over low heat. Spray a small, shallow baking dish with nonstick cooking spray and place chicken breasts in dish.

Mix water with spaghetti sauce and stir. Pour over chicken breasts. Cover the top of chicken and sauce with shredded mozzarella cheese and bake at 350 degrees for 35 to 40 minutes.

Each serving provides:

276	Calories	1.42 g	Fat
33.71 g	Protein	882 g	Sodium
31.21 g	Carbohydrate	54.01 mg	Cholesterol

Diabetic exchanges: Very lean meat, 4; vegetable, 2; starch, 1

MAIN DISHES

Cheese and Spinach Calzone

¼ cup frozen chopped spinach, thawed,
   with moisture pressed out
¾ cup 1 percent cottage cheese, drained
2 teaspoons dry onion flakes
2 tablespoons fat-free Parmesan cheese
¼ teaspoon garlic powder
1 tablespoon fat-free liquid egg product
¼ cup lowfat mozzarella cheese
1 tablespoon fat-free Italian salad dressing
½ can of rolled, refrigerated pizza dough

Preheat oven to 375 degrees.

Combine all ingredients, except pizza dough, in medium bowl and mix thoroughly with a spoon.

Unroll pizza dough and cut in half. Store the other half in the refrigerator for another recipe, or make yourself a small pizza with it the next day. Cut the half you are using in half. Stretch and roll each piece until it is big enough to accommodate half of the filling mixture. Spray baking sheet or pan with nonstick cooking spray.

Fill each rolled-out piece of dough with half of the filling mixture and fold dough over the top of mixture, to form sort of a half-moon shape. Pinch all edges tightly with your fingers or a fork to seal the filling in. Place on baking sheet and bake at 375 degrees for 20 to 25 minutes.

Each serving provides:

314	Calories	3.92 g	Fat
24.21 g	Protein	915 g	Sodium
41.85 g	Carbohydrate	10.25 mg	Cholesterol

Diabetic exchanges: Very lean meat, 3; vegetable, 2; starch, 2

Chicken Tetrazzini

SERVES 4

1 boneless, skinless chicken breast (4 ounces),
   cut into small chunks
½ cup fat-free cream cheese
¾ cup chicken broth
1 can (4 ounces) sliced mushrooms, drained
½ cup Campbell's 98 percent fat-free
   cream of mushroom soup
1 cup Kraft fat-free shredded mozzarella cheese
   (½ cup for topping and ½ cup for mixing in recipe)
½ teaspoon Molly McButter butter sprinkles
2 teaspoons dry onion flakes
   Salt and black pepper to taste
3 cups cooked spaghetti

Preheat oven to 350 degrees.

Spray small skillet with nonstick cooking spray. Brown and cook chicken pieces in skillet until tender. Set aside.

In medium bowl, whip cream cheese with electric mixer until smooth. Gradually add chicken broth and continue until thoroughly mixed. Add mushrooms, mushroom soup, ½ cup mozzarella cheese, Molly McButter, dry onion flakes, and salt and black pepper. Stir and mix with spoon, then add cooked chicken pieces.

Mix this mixture with the cooked spaghetti and stir with spoon. Spray medium baking dish, about 8-inch square, with nonstick cooking spray. Pour entire mixture into dish and top with the other ½ cup of shredded mozzarella. Bake at 350 degrees for about 25 minutes.

Each serving provides:

281	Calories	1.88 g	Fat
26.80 g	Protein	1045 g	Sodium
37.65 g	Carbohydrate	24.73 mg	Cholesterol

Diabetic exchanges: Very lean meat, 3; vegetable, ½; starch, 2

Cheese Manicotti

6 manicotti shells, cooked*
½ cup 1 percent cottage cheese, drained thoroughly
½ cup Kraft fat-free shredded mozzarella cheese
½ cup shredded Parmesan cheese
2 tablespoons fat-free liquid egg product
⅛ teaspoon garlic powder
1 tablespoon dry onion flakes
  Black pepper to taste
1 can (14½ ounces) chopped tomatoes
⅛ teaspoon dry oregano flakes
½ cup fat-free chicken broth

Preheat oven to 375 degrees.

*Cook 1 or 2 extra shells, in case 1 splits or breaks. Cook in boiling water for 4 minutes. Drain, per package instructions.

In medium bowl, combine cottage cheese, mozzarella, and Parmesan cheese. Add liquid egg product, garlic powder, onion flakes, and black pepper. Mix with spoon.

Spray 9-inch square glass baking dish with nonstick cooking spray. Stuff and pack each manicotti shell with cheese mixture. Place in baking dish and stuff remaining shells.

In medium bowl, combine tomatoes, oregano, and chicken broth. Gently spoon this mixture over the top of the stuffed manicotti. Cover with aluminum foil and bake for 1 hour at 375 degrees. Cook an extra 10 minutes uncovered.

Each serving provides:

245	Calories	3.24 g	Fat
20.40 g	Protein	696 g	Sodium
34.04 g	Carbohydrate	10.33 mg	Cholesterol

Diabetic exchanges: Very lean meat, 3; vegetable, ½; starch, 1½

Cheese Ravioli with Olive Sauce

SERVES 4

1 package (9 ounces) refrigerated-type light cheese ravioli
1 small onion, chopped
2 cloves garlic, pressed
2 tablespoons red cooking wine
1 can (14½ ounces) tomato sauce
⅛ teaspoon dry oregano
2 teaspoons dry onion flakes
1 cup fat-free chicken broth
¼ teaspoon onion powder
   Salt and black pepper to taste
⅓ cup salad olives, drained
1 tablespoon olive juice from jar

Cook ravioli according to package directions, after sauce is done.

Spray medium saucepan with nonstick cooking spray. Add onion, garlic, and cooking wine. Simmer over low heat until onion is lightly browned. Add tomato sauce, oregano, dry onion flakes, chicken broth, onion powder, and salt and black pepper. Simmer, uncovered, over low heat for 15 to 20 minutes. Stir occasionally. Remove from heat and add olives and olive juice. Stir and serve over cooked ravioli.

Each serving provides:

220	Calories	4.42 g	Fat
12.16 g	Protein	1542 g	Sodium
34.53 g	Carbohydrate	0 mg	Cholesterol

Diabetic exchanges: Very lean meat, 1; starch, 2; fat, ½

Eggplant Lasagna

4 lasagna noodles
1 small eggplant, peeled and sliced
1 cup 1 percent cottage cheese
⅓ cup fat-free liquid egg product
½ cup fat-free sour cream
1 cup lowfat pasta sauce
2 cloves garlic, pressed
¼ bell pepper, sliced in long thin pieces
1 small onion, chopped
2 tablespoons water
½ cup shredded fat-free mozzarella cheese
¼ cup fat-free Parmesan cheese

Preheat oven to 350 degrees.

Cook lasagna according to package directions, drain, and cool.

Place eggplant slices on paper towels and let stand until ready to use.

In medium bowl, combine cottage cheese, egg product, and sour cream, and stir until well blended.

In another bowl, combine pasta sauce, garlic, bell pepper, onion, and water. Stir with a spoon until blended.

Spray a medium baking dish with nonstick cooking spray. I like a glass loaf pan. Layer all ingredients in casserole in alternating layers, beginning with the eggplant. Remember the grated cheese and top with fat-free Parmesan cheese. Bake 1 hour at 350 degrees.

Each serving provides:

186	Calories	.84 g	Fat
15.05 g	Protein	432 g	Sodium
29.35 g	Carbohydrate	5.34 mg	Cholesterol

Diabetic exchanges: Very lean meat, 2; vegetable, 1; starch, 1

Cheery Polenta with Red Sauce

4   slices polenta, about ½-inch thick (I buy mine in a roll at the supermarket.)
1   small onion, chopped
1   teaspoon Molly McButter butter sprinkles
1   cup tomato sauce
1   clove garlic, pressed
¼   teaspoon onion powder
1   tablespoon red cooking wine
⅓   cup fat-free chicken broth
⅛   teaspoon Italian seasoning
2   tablespoons fat-free Parmesan cheese
¾   cup shredded Healthy Choice lowfat mozzarella cheese

Preheat oven to 350 degrees.

Spray medium skillet with nonstick cooking spray. Place polenta slices in skillet and brown on each side.

Spray small skillet with nonstick cooking spray. Add onion and Molly McButter, and simmer onion until tender.

In small saucepan, combine tomato sauce, garlic, onion powder, red cooking wine, chicken broth, and Italian seasoning. Stir and simmer over low heat until onion and polenta are done.

Spray glass pie plate with nonstick cooking spray. Line bottom of pie plate with cooked onion. Sprinkle Parmesan cheese over onion. Place browned slices of polenta in pie plate on top of onion. Sprinkle shredded mozzarella cheese over polenta. Spoon sauce over the top and bake at 350 degrees for 15 to 18 minutes.

Each serving provides:

240	Calories	2.59 g	Fat
17.85 g	Protein	1744 g	Sodium
35.11 g	Carbohydrate	7.50 mg	Cholesterol

Diabetic exchanges: Very lean meat, 2; vegetable, 3; starch, 1

Zucchini and Tomato Casserole

SERVES 6

2 medium-small zucchini, sliced about ½-inch thick
1 medium onion, sliced
1 can (14½ ounces) chopped tomatoes,
    drained thoroughly
1½ cups 1 percent cottage cheese, drained
⅓ cup fat-free liquid egg product
2 slices roasted bell pepper, cut into small pieces
1 clove garlic, pressed
    Salt and black pepper to taste

Preheat oven to 350 degrees.

Spray 9-inch square glass baking dish with nonstick cooking spray. Layer bottom of baking dish with sliced zucchini. Next, add a layer of sliced onion, then chopped tomatoes.

In medium bowl, combine cottage cheese, egg product, roasted bell peppers, and garlic. Add salt and black pepper, and stir with spoon. Pour this mixture in baking dish, over zucchini and onion. Bake, uncovered, at 350 degrees for 45 to 50 minutes.

Each serving provides:

85	Calories	.92 g	Fat
10.31 g	Protein	453 g	Sodium
9.61 g	Carbohydrate	2.50 mg	Cholesterol

Diabetic exchanges: Very lean meat, 1; vegetable, 2

Ziti with Mushrooms and Tomato

SERVES 3

2 cups fresh sliced mushrooms
1 small onion, chopped
2 cloves garlic, pressed
1 tablespoon Molly McButter butter sprinkles
1 cup tomato sauce
¼ teaspoon oregano
¼ teaspoon red pepper flakes
  Garlic salt and black pepper to taste
6 tablespoons fancy shredded Parmesan cheese,
  for garnish
1½ cups cooked ziti pasta

Spray medium skillet with nonstick cooking spray. Add mushrooms, onion, garlic, and Molly McButter; stir over medium heat for 6 to 8 minutes. Add tomato sauce, oregano, red pepper flakes, and garlic salt and black pepper. Simmer over low heat for 8 to 10 minutes. Add cooked ziti pasta and stir another 1 or 2 minutes. Garnish each serving with 2 tablespoons shredded Parmesan cheese.

Each serving provides:

206	Calories	3.90 g	Fat
10.17 g	Protein	861 g	Sodium
33.42 g	Carbohydrate	8.0 mg	Cholesterol

Diabetic exchanges: Lean meat, 1; vegetable, 2; starch, 1¼

Tortellini with Sour Cream and Sun-Dried Tomato

SERVES 4

      2 green onions, sliced
      1 clove garlic, pressed
  2½ cups fat-free chicken broth
      2 sun-dried tomatoes, cut into small pieces
      1 teaspoon Molly McButter butter sprinkles
        Salt and black pepper to taste
    ½ cup fat-free sour cream
    ⅓ cup shredded Parmesan cheese, for garnish
      1 package (9 ounces) refrigerated-type light cheese
        tortellini, cooked according to package directions

Spray medium saucepan with nonstick cooking spray. Add green onions and garlic, and brown lightly. Add chicken broth, tomato pieces, and Molly McButter. Simmer over low heat for 12 to 15 minutes. Add salt and black pepper. Using a whisk, blend sour cream into mixture. Remove from heat and serve over cooked tortellini. (Serve in a bowl instead of a plate, because sauce is thin.) Garnish with shredded Parmesan.

Each serving provides:

201	Calories	3.64 g	Fat
12.78 g	Protein	1012 g	Sodium
26.64 g	Carbohydrate	23.93 mg	Cholesterol

Diabetic exchanges: Very lean meat, 1; starch, 2

Eggplant Parmesan

1   small eggplant, peeled and sliced in ½-inch slices
1   egg white, slightly beaten
1   cup crushed corn flakes
½   cup fat-free Parmesan cheese
½   cup Kraft fat-free mozzarella shredded cheese
1   cup stewed, chopped tomatoes
1   small onion, chopped
1   teaspoon garlic powder
     Salt and black pepper to taste

Preheat oven to 350 degrees.

Spray large skillet with nonstick cooking spray. Dip each eggplant slice in egg white and then both sides in corn flakes. Brown lightly in skillet.

Spray medium casserole dish with nonstick cooking spray. Place browned eggplant slices in baking dish. Sprinkle with Parmesan and mozzarella cheese. Gently pour tomatoes over entire casserole. Sprinkle onion over top, and season with garlic powder, and salt and black pepper. Bake at 350 degrees for 45 to 50 minutes.

Each serving provides:

136	Calories	.45 g	Fat
7.14 g	Protein	412 g	Sodium
25.55 g	Carbohydrate	5.67 mg	Cholesterol

Diabetic exchanges: Very lean meat, 1; vegetable, 2; starch, ½

Angel Hair Pasta with Carmelized Onions

1 large sweet onion, sliced
Juice of 1 lemon
½ cup fat-free chicken broth
½ teaspoon garlic salt
⅛ teaspoon onion powder
Black pepper to taste
1 teaspoon Molly McButter butter sprinkles
1 cup skim milk
1½ cups cooked angel hair pasta
4 tablespoons shredded Parmesan cheese

Spray large skillet with nonstick cooking spray. Add sliced onion, cover with lid, and cook over medium-low heat until onion is done. Uncover and carefully brown onion. Squeeze lemon juice over onion. These burn easily, so watch closely. Once onion is browned, pour in chicken broth and simmer about 5 minutes. Add all remaining ingredients and stir over low heat for 1 to 2 minutes. Serve over angel hair pasta. Garnish with Parmesan cheese when serving.

	Each serving provides:		
145	Calories	2.05 g	Fat
7.70 g	Protein	531 g	Sodium
23.98 g	Carbohydrate	5.0 mg	Cholesterol

Diabetic exchanges: Vegetable, 2; starch, 1; skim milk, ¼

Tortellini with Roasted Sweet Pepper Sauce

SERVES 3

1 small onion, chopped
1 can (4 ounces) tomato sauce
½ cup fat-free chicken broth
½ cup "Mezzetta" brand roasted yellow and
    red sweet peppers (7.25 ounces jar)
2 cloves garlic, pressed
1 tablespoon red cooking wine
⅛ teaspoon Italian seasoning
    Garlic salt to taste
    Black pepper to taste
1½ cups cooked cheese tortellini

Spray medium saucepan with nonstick cooking spray. Add onion and brown over medium-low heat. Add all remaining ingredients, except tortellini. Simmer and cook over low heat for 5 to 8 minutes.

Serve over cooked tortellini.

Each serving provides:

196	Calories	2.49 g	Fat
8.22 g	Protein	721 g	Sodium
35.87 g	Carbohydrate	12.50 mg	Cholesterol

Diabetic exchanges: Vegetable, 1½; starch, 2

4

Vegetables

Oven-Roasted Garlic

SERVES 4

  2 whole heads fresh garlic
½ cup red cooking wine
1½ tablespoons Molly McButter butter sprinkles

Preheat oven to 375 degrees.

Slice across and cut about a third off the top of each head of garlic. All, or almost all, of the cloves in each head should be exposed. Place both heads of garlic in a small baking dish and pour wine over each exposed head. Sprinkle each head with Molly McButter. Cover and bake for about 1 hour. Check a couple of times during baking and add a little water if dish is getting too dry.

    Serve warm with lowfat bread or crackers.

Each serving provides:

48	Calories	.16 g	Fat
1.52 g	Protein	301 g	Sodium
9.15 g	Carbohydrate	0 mg	Cholesterol

Diabetic exchanges: Vegetable, 2

Stuffed Potatoes with Garlic

Serves 4

2   medium baking potatoes, washed and baked in oven
2   green onions, sliced
4   cloves garlic, pressed
1   tablespoon Molly McButter butter sprinkles
    Garlic salt and black pepper to taste
¼   cup fat-free sour cream
1   tablespoon sliced black olives
4   tablespoons shredded Parmesan cheese

Preheat oven to 375 degrees.

After potatoes are baked, set aside to cool. When cool enough to handle, carefully slice in half lengthwise. Using a spoon, hollow out the centers of the potato halves. Place potato insides in a medium bowl.

Spray small skillet with nonstick cooking spray and brown onion and garlic lightly. Add onion and garlic to bowl with potato and add all other ingredients, except olives and Parmesan cheese. Whip with electric mixer until smooth. Add a few tablespoons of skim milk while whipping, if needed for moisture. Fold in olives and mix with spoon.

Fill potato shells with potato mixture and bake at 375 degrees for 15 to 20 minutes. Remove and garnish each potato with shredded Parmesan cheese and serve.

	Each serving provides:		
155	Calories	1.90 g	Fat
5.68 g	Protein	269 g	Sodium
29.29 g	Carbohydrate	4.0 mg	Cholesterol
	Diabetic exchanges: Starch, 2		

Roasted Eggplant
with Parmesan Cheese

SERVES 4

4 slices (¾-inch) peeled eggplant
   Garlic salt to taste
½ teaspoon Molly McButter butter sprinkles
   Black pepper to taste
4 tablespoons canned tomato sauce
½ cup Kraft fat-free shredded mozzarella cheese
2 tablespoons fancy shredded Parmesan cheese

Spray baking dish or pan with nonstick cooking spray. Line bottom of pan with sliced eggplant. Place under broiler and brown on one side; turn, and brown on the other side. Remove from broiler, sprinkle with garlic salt, Molly McButter, and black pepper to taste. Return to broiler under low heat, but move several inches away from heat, so it will cook slower. Cook until eggplant is tender to fork.

Remove eggplant from oven and place 1 tablespoon of tomato sauce on top of each piece and spread around with a spoon. Sprinkle mozzarella cheese on top of each slice of eggplant and top with a light sprinkle of Parmesan. Place back under broiler long enough to melt cheese. Serve warm and enjoy.

Each serving provides:

53	Calories	.88 g	Fat
6.32 g	Protein	263 g	Sodium
5.28 g	Carbohydrate	4.50 mg	Cholesterol

Diabetic exchanges: Very lean meat, 1; vegetable, 1

Roasted Italian Carrots and Potatoes

 1 large potato, peeled and cut into wedges
12 whole baby carrots
 1 small onion, cut in chunks
 3 tablespoons fat-free zesty Italian salad dressing
½ cup fat-free chicken broth
½ teaspoon dry ranch dressing mix
    Garlic salt to taste
    Black pepper to taste

Preheat oven to 400 degrees.

Place vegetables in medium glass bowl. Cover and cook in microwave on high for 3 minutes. Stir and cook 3 more minutes.

In small bowl, combine Italian dressing and chicken broth.

Spray medium baking dish with nonstick cooking spray. Add vegetables to baking dish and spoon dressing mixture over the vegetables. Sprinkle over top: ranch dressing mix, garlic salt, and black pepper. Cover and bake at 400 degrees for 40 to 45 minutes. Uncover for the last 15 minutes to let vegetables brown.

Each serving provides:

58	Calories	.13 g	Fat	
1.62 g	Protein	357 g	Sodium	
12.86 g	Carbohydrate	0 mg	Cholesterol	

Diabetic exchanges: Vegetable, 1½; starch, ¼

Marsala Mushrooms with Onions

SERVES 4

1 small onion, sliced
3 cups raw, whole mushrooms
¼ cup marsala cooking wine (found in most supermarkets)
½ cup fat-free chicken broth
1 tablespoon Molly McButter butter sprinkles
1 clove garlic, pressed
   Black pepper to taste

Spray medium skillet or saucepan with nonstick cooking spray. Add onion, and stir and cook over medium-low heat until onion is lightly browned. Add all remaining ingredients and simmer, covered, for 5 minutes. Uncover and cook until almost all the liquid is cooked away. Stir often. Serve as a side dish or appetizer.

Each serving provides:

46	Calories	.29 g	Fat
1.79 g	Protein	351 g	Sodium
8.30 g	Carbohydrate	0 mg	Cholesterol

Diabetic exchanges: Vegetable, 2

Garlic Mashed Potatoes

SERVES 3

4 cloves fresh peeled garlic
½ cup white cooking wine
2 tablespoons Molly McButter butter sprinkles
1 large potato, peeled and cut into chunks
1½ tablespoons evaporated skim milk
   Salt and black pepper to taste

In small saucepan, simmer garlic, cooking wine, and 1 tablespoon Molly McButter. Cover and cook over low heat for
about 20 minutes, or until garlic is tender. Add 1 or 2 tablespoons of water if pan becomes too dry.

Place potato chunks in medium saucepan, cover with
water, and cook until tender, 20 to 25 minutes. Drain water
from potatoes and add evaporated milk, 1 tablespoon Molly
McButter, and salt and black pepper. Mash potatoes with
electric mixer. Using a dinner fork, mash heads of garlic. Add
garlic to mashed potatoes and mix until smooth.

Each serving provides:

80	Calories	.11	g	Fat
1.77 g	Protein	493	g	Sodium
15.16 g	Carbohydrate	.31	mg	Cholesterol

Diabetic exchanges: Starch, 1

Creamed Garlic Potatoes

8 small new potatoes, cut in half and cooked
2 cloves garlic, pressed
¼ cup white cooking wine

White Sauce
½ cup skim milk
1 tablespoon flour
½ cup fat-free chicken broth
¼ cup fat-free sour cream
1 teaspoon Molly McButter butter sprinkles
   Salt and black pepper to taste

Cook new potatoes and set aside. Drain before using.

In skillet, sauté garlic in ¼ cup white cooking wine. Set aside while making white sauce.

In small bowl, whisk together milk and flour until smooth. Add all remaining ingredients and stir. Pour this mixture into small saucepan and stir over medium-low heat until sauce starts to thicken. Set aside.

Add potatoes to garlic in skillet and begin to simmer, adding white sauce. Simmer 2 minutes and serve.

Each serving provides:

106	Calories	.15 g	Fat
3.29 g	Protein	195 g	Sodium
21.77 g	Carbohydrate	.33 mg	Cholesterol

Diabetic exchanges: Vegetable, 1; starch, 1

Italian Roasted Vegetables

10 fresh whole baby carrots, peeled
 1 medium potato, peeled and cut into long wedges
 1 small onion, cut into chunks
⅓ cup fat-free chicken broth
⅓ cup fat-free Italian salad dressing
¼ teaspoon garlic powder or salt
½ teaspoon dry ranch dressing mix
½ teaspoon Molly McButter butter sprinkles
   Black pepper to taste

Preheat oven to 400 degrees.

Microwave vegetables in a covered container for 3 minutes on high. Stir and cook another 3 minutes. Let stand while preparing other ingredients.

In small bowl, combine chicken broth, Italian dressing, garlic powder, dry ranch dressing mix, and Molly McButter. Stir until well blended.

Spray medium baking dish with nonstick cooking spray. Pour vegetables into dish and spoon chicken broth mixture over all vegetables. Add black pepper to taste. Cover and bake in oven at 400 degrees, 35 to 40 minutes, or until vegetables are tender.

Each serving provides:

60	Calories	.13 g	Fat
1.53 g	Protein	524 g	Sodium
12.93 g	Carbohydrate	0 mg	Cholesterol

Diabetic exchanges: Vegetable, 2; starch, 1/4

Baked Artichokes
with Lemon Cream Sauce

SERVES 4

1 can (14 ounces) water-packed artichoke hearts, drained
1 teaspoon Molly McButter butter sprinkles
2 tablespoons lemon juice

Sauce
½ cup fat-free cream cheese
2 teaspoons lemon juice, warmed
½ teaspoon Molly McButter butter sprinkles
¼ teaspoon fresh lemon peel, grated
4 tablespoons shredded Parmesan cheese

Preheat oven to 375 degrees.

Spray small baking dish with nonstick cooking spray. Place drained artichoke hearts in dish and pour lemon juice over the top. Sprinkle on Molly McButter. Bake in oven for 25 to 30 minutes. While artichokes are baking, prepare sauce. Combine lemon juice and Molly McButter. Gently warm the lemon juice enough for Molly McButter to melt and stir until well blended. Using a medium bowl, combine all ingredients for sauce, including lemon juice and Molly McButter. Mix with electric mixer until smooth.

Pour sauce over artichokes just before serving. Garnish with shredded Parmesan cheese. Enjoy!

Each serving provides:

94	Calories	1.73 g	Fat
9.54 g	Protein	611 g	Sodium
10.72 g	Carbohydrate	6.64 mg	Cholesterol

Diabetic exchanges: Very lean meat, 2; vegetable, 1

5

Pizzas and Breads

Sweet Italian Sausage Mini Pizza

SERVES 2

1   link sweet Italian turkey sausage, sliced
½   small onion, chopped
1   tablespoon lowfat pasta sauce
1   Italian-style mini pizza crust
⅛   teaspoon garlic powder to taste
½   cup Kraft fat-free mozzarella cheese

Preheat oven to 400 degrees.

Spray small skillet with nonstick cooking spray. Add sliced sausage and onion, and brown and simmer over low heat until done. Set aside.

Spread pasta sauce over mini pizza. Sprinkle on garlic powder, then add sausage and onion. Top with mozzarella cheese and place on baking sheet, sprayed with nonstick cooking spray. Cook at 400 degrees for 7 to 10 minutes, or until cheese is melted.

Each serving provides:

266	Calories	6.06 g	Fat
22.52 g	Protein	944 g	Sodium
28.90 g	Carbohydrate	30.0 mg	Cholesterol

Diabetic exchanges: Very lean meat, 3; starch, 2

Prosciutto and Pineapple Mini Pizza

SERVES 2

2 tablespoons chopped onion
1 tablespoon green pepper, finely chopped
1 small (about 6-inch) Italian-style pizza shell
1 tablespoon lowfat pasta sauce
2 slices of prosciutto
2 tablespoons crushed pineapple
⅓ cup lowfat mozzarella cheese, grated

Preheat oven to 425 degrees.

Spray small skillet with nonstick cooking spray. Add onion and green pepper, and simmer until tender. Add a little water if skillet gets too dry. After cooking, set aside.

Spray small baking sheet or pan with nonstick cooking spray. Place pizza shell on baking sheet. Spread pasta sauce evenly over pizza shell with spoon. Next, lay the 2 slices of prosciutto to cover top of pizza. Add onion, green pepper, and pineapple. Distribute each layer evenly. Sprinkle cheese on top.

Place in oven at 425 degrees for 10 to 15 minutes. Serve hot.

Each serving provides:

242	Calories	6.37 g	Fat
16.48 g	Protein	623 g	Sodium
29.17 g	Carbohydrate	17.16 mg	Cholesterol

Diabetic exchanges: Lean meat, 1; very lean meat, 1; starch, 2

Pesto Mini Pizza

SERVES 2

1 individual-sized Boboli pizza crust
2 teaspoons pesto, already prepared
½ cup fat-free Kraft shredded mozzarella cheese
1 small tomato, sliced
3 strips roasted bell pepper, cut in half
  Light sprinkling of oregano
  Garlic salt to taste
  Light sprinkling of crushed red pepper flakes
¼ cup shredded Parmesan cheese

Preheat oven to 400 degrees.

Spread pesto on Boboli crust. Spread mozzarella cheese evenly over crust. Then add sliced tomato. Next, add pieces of roasted bell pepper, oregano, garlic salt, and crushed red pepper flakes. Top with shredded Parmesan cheese. Bake in oven at 400 degrees for 15 minutes.

Each serving provides:

267	Calories	8.12 g	Fat
20.02 g	Protein	780 g	Sodium
29.0 g	Carbohydrate	13.0 mg	Cholesterol

Diabetic exchanges: Lean meat, 2; starch, 2

Artichoke and Basil Mini Pizza

1 individual-sized Boboli pizza crust
1 tablespoon fresh basil, chopped
¾ cup water-packed, quartered, small artichoke hearts, cut in half
½ cup Kraft fat-free shredded mozzarella cheese
    Garlic salt to taste
¼ cup shredded Parmesan cheese

Preheat oven to 400 degrees.

Sprinkle chopped fresh basil on mini pizza crust. Add drained artichoke pieces, then sprinkle on mozzarella cheese. Add garlic salt to taste and top with shredded Parmesan cheese.

Bake at 400 degrees for 15 minutes.

Each serving provides:

259	Calories	6.15 g	Fat
20.69 g	Protein	877 g	Sodium
30.44 g	Carbohydrate	13.0 mg	Cholesterol

Diabetic exchanges: Very lean meat, 2; vegetable, 1; starch, 2

Mini Pizza with Feta and Sun-Dried Tomatoes

½ cup chopped, cooked onion
2 tablespoons tomato sauce
1 tablespoon fresh basil, chopped
1 clove garlic, pressed
⅛ teaspoon dry oregano flakes
1 individual-sized Boboli pizza crust
4 sun-dried tomatoes, cut into small pieces
½ cup lowfat feta cheese
  Salt and black pepper to taste

Preheat oven to 400 degrees.

Brown onion in small skillet sprayed with nonstick cooking spray.

In small bowl, combine tomato sauce, basil, garlic, salt, black pepper, and oregano. Spread this mixture over pizza crust. Next, arrange pieces of sun-dried tomatoes over sauce, then add browned onion evenly. Top with feta cheese.

Spray baking sheet with nonstick cooking spray. Place pizza on baking sheet and bake at 400 degrees for 15 minutes.

Each serving provides:

208	Calories	4.76 g	Fat
9.88 g	Protein	673 g	Sodium
32.39 g	Carbohydrate	5.0 mg	Cholesterol

Diabetic exchanges: Lean meat, 1; starch, 2

Mini Pizza with Marinated Artichoke Hearts

SERVES 2

1 small onion, thinly sliced
1 small (6-inch) Italian-style pizza shell
1 tablespoon lowfat pasta sauce
½ cup Gourmet Award marinated and
  quartered artichoke hearts*
⅓ cup Healthy Choice grated lowfat mozzarella cheese
  Garlic salt to taste

*I used this particular brand because it was lower in fat.

Preheat oven to 425 degrees.

Spray small skillet with nonstick cooking spray. Add sliced onion, and brown and simmer until done. Add a little water if needed to keep from sticking or burning. When onion is done, set aside.

Spray small baking sheet or pan with nonstick cooking spray. Place pizza shell on pan. Add pasta sauce to pizza shell and spread with a spoon to distribute evenly.

Add artichoke hearts evenly over top. Repeat with cooked onion slices. Sprinkle grated cheese on top and sprinkle top of cheese with garlic salt if desired.

Place in oven at 425 degrees for 10 to 15 minutes. Serve hot.

Each serving provides:

235	Calories	5.62 g	Fat
12.98 g	Protein	586 g	Sodium
34.02 g	Carbohydrate	2.0 mg	Cholesterol

Diabetic exchanges: Lean meat, 1; vegetable, 1; starch, 2

Broccoli and Cheese Pizza

2 cloves garlic, pressed
1 teaspoon Molly McButter butter sprinkles
¼ cup chicken broth
¾ cup fresh broccoli, cut into small pieces
1 individual-sized Boboli pizza crust
½ cup Kraft fat-free shredded mozzarella cheese
¼ cup Kraft fat-free shredded American or
   Cheddar cheese
4 tablespoons shredded Parmesan cheese

Preheat oven to 400 degrees.

Spray small saucepan with nonstick cooking spray. Add garlic, Molly McButter, chicken broth, and broccoli. Cook and stir over medium-low heat until most of the liquid has cooked away. There should be about 1 tablespoon left. Arrange this mixture on pizza crust, then add the mozzarella and American or Cheddar cheese. Top with shredded Parmesan cheese and bake in oven at 400 degrees for 15 minutes.

Each serving provides:

274	Calories	6.13 g	Fat
23.99 g	Protein	1136 g	Sodium
31.41 g	Carbohydrate	13.0 mg	Cholesterol

Diabetic exchanges: Very lean meat, 3; vegetable, 2; starch, 1½

Caramelized Onion
Mini Pizza with Pine Nuts

SERVES 2

1 medium onion, thinly sliced
2 tablespoons pine nuts, coarsely chopped
½ teaspoon Molly McButter butter sprinkles
1 tablespoon lowfat pizza or pasta sauce
1 Italian-style mini pizza crust (Choose the brand with the lowest fat.)
 Garlic salt to taste
½ cup Kraft fat-free shredded mozzarella cheese

Preheat oven to 400 degrees.

Spray small skillet with nonstick cooking spray. Add onion; brown and cook until onion is tender and has a pretty golden brown color. Add chopped pine nuts and Molly McButter, and stir until pine nuts are browned slightly.

Spray baking sheet with nonstick cooking spray. Spread 1 tablespoon of pasta sauce over mini pizza. Sprinkle on garlic salt. Add onion and pine nut mixture evenly over top. Sprinkle on the mozzarella. Place mini pizza on baking sheet and bake at 400 degrees for 7 to 10 minutes, or until cheese melts.

Each serving provides:

275	Calories	8.22 g	Fat
18.43 g	Protein	579 g	Sodium
34.31 g	Carbohydrate	5.0 mg	Cholesterol

Diabetic exchanges: Very lean meat, 2; starch, 2; fat, 1

Zesty Italian Pizza Roll

1 can (10 ounces) refrigerated pizza dough
⅓ cup fat-free cream cheese
4 slices lowfat ham
½ cup roasted bell peppers (available in a jar)
1 tablespoon sliced salad olives
1 cup Kraft fat-free shredded mozzarella cheese
2 tablespoons fat-free zesty Italian salad dressing
  Garlic powder to taste
½ teaspoon poppy seeds

Preheat oven to 400 degrees.

Remove pizza dough from roll and spread on clean dry surface. Use a rolling pin or your fingers to make dough bigger. Keep dough in somewhat of a rectangular shape for rolling later.

Starting at the edge closest to you, spread cream cheese across the dough, then add two slices of ham. Roll the edge of the dough over the ham and cream cheese. Next, add roasted bell peppers and salad olives and roll dough. Add cheese and half the Italian dressing. Roll the dough and then add more ham slices, garlic powder, salad olives, and Italian dressing. Finish rolling dough into long roll.

Spray baking sheet with nonstick cooking spray. Place roll on baking sheet and sprinkle poppy seeds over the top of the roll. Bake at 400 degrees for 23 to 25 minutes. Allow to cool slightly before slicing and serving.

Each serving provides:

105	Calories	1.09 g	Fat
7.96 g	Protein	370 g	Sodium
14.62 g	Carbohydrate	4.37 mg	Cholesterol

Diabetic exchanges: Very lean meat, 1; starch, 1

Apple Cinnamon Mini Pizza

1   medium apple, peeled and thinly sliced
½   teaspoon ground cinnamon
2   teaspoons Molly McButter butter sprinkles
1   individual-sized lowfat pizza crust
6   packets Equal sweetener, added after cooking

Preheat oven to 400 degrees.

Place apple slices in small saucepan with ¼ cup water. Cover and cook over medium-low heat until apple slices are tender, 8 to 10 minutes. Uncover and simmer until about 2 tablespoons of the water is left. Add cinnamon and Molly McButter and remove from heat.

Arrange apple slices on mini pizza crust and drizzle any liquid over the top of the apples. Bake at 400 degrees for 15 to 18 minutes. Remove from the oven and sprinkle on the 6 packets of Equal.

Each serving provides:

103	Calories	1.61 g	Fat
4.56 g	Protein	245 g	Sodium
17.73 g	Carbohydrate	0 mg	Cholesterol

Diabetic exchanges: Starch, 1; fruit, ½

Sweet Italian Sausage and Cheese Roll

2 links sweet Italian turkey sausage, sliced
1 can (10 ounces) refrigerated pizza dough
1 large onion, sliced
1 clove garlic, pressed
½ cup roasted red and yellow sweet peppers
1 cup Kraft fat-free shredded mozzarella cheese
½ teaspoon fennel seed
2 tablespoons fat-free Zesty Italian dressing
   Salt and black pepper to taste
1 teaspoon sesame seeds

Preheat oven to 375 degrees.

Spray small skillet with nonstick cooking spray. Brown and cook sliced Italian sausage. Set aside to cool.

Spread pizza dough on clean dry surface and roll or spread to enlarge surface. Using all ingredients, except sesame seeds, starting from the side of dough that is closest to you, add an ingredient and roll. On some items, such as the Italian dressing, you might want to add half and roll; then add the next ingredient and repeat until all ingredients are used. Finish rolling dough and place on baking sheet sprayed with nonstick cooking spray. Sprinkle top of roll with sesame seeds. Bake at 375 degrees for 15 to 20 minutes, or until golden brown.

Each serving provides:

125		Calories	2.22	g	Fat
9.18	g	Protein	451	g	Sodium
15.79	g	Carbohydrate	12.0	mg	Cholesterol

Diabetic exchanges: Lean meat, 1; starch, 1

Pepperoni Cheese Bread

SERVES 12

½ cup onion, chopped
1 tablespoon Molly McButter butter sprinkles
3 tablespoons water
1 roll refrigerated pizza dough
⅓ cup shredded Parmesan cheese
1½ cups fat-free Kraft shredded mozzarella cheese
10 pieces turkey pepperoni
   Garlic salt to taste
2 tablespoons fat-free liquid egg product
   Butter-flavored cooking spray

Preheat oven to 350 degrees.

Brown onion in skillet sprayed with nonstick cooking spray. After onion is browned, add 3 tablespoons water and 1 tablespoon Molly McButter, and stir until mixed thoroughly. Set aside to cool.

Remove pizza dough from can and spread on clean surface. Using a rolling pin, roll out dough. Begin covering surface evenly with cheeses, pepperoni, onion mixture, and garlic salt. Use the liquid that is with the onion. Begin at the edge of the long side and roll dough. After a couple of rolls, fold each end inside, as you would an egg roll. Continue rolling until completely rolled up. Place on baking sheet, sprayed with nonstick cooking spray.

Pinch together all seams and edges, then brush the top with fat-free liquid egg product. Spray top of loaf with butter-flavored cooking spray. Bake in oven at 350 degrees for 30 minutes. Remove and let loaf cool a little before slicing. Two slices equal 1 serving.

Each serving provides:

100	Calories	1.56 g	Fat
8.23 g	Protein	331 g	Sodium
12.40 g	Carbohydrate	6.24 mg	Cholesterol

Diabetic exchanges: Very lean meat, 1; starch, ¾

Open-Faced Italian Sandwich

SERVES 4

⅓ cup chopped onion
1 clove garlic, pressed
¼ cup white cooking wine
1 link Italian turkey sausage, cut into small pieces
¼ cup fat-free chicken broth
½ cup fresh sliced mushrooms
½ medium red or yellow bell pepper, thinly sliced
1 small tomato, chopped
   Salt and black pepper to taste
¾ cup Kraft fat-free shredded mozzarella cheese
4 slices bread, toasted

Spray skillet with olive oil spray. Stir and cook the onion and garlic in white wine over medium-low heat, 5 to 6 minutes. Add remaining ingredients, except cheese and bread. Simmer and stir for 10 minutes.

Spoon mixture over each slice of toast. Sprinkle cheese on top and place under broiler until cheese melts. Watch carefully. This burns easily.

Each serving provides:

175	Calories	3.06 g	Fat
12.84 g	Protein	796 g	Sodium
20.34 g	Carbohydrate	22.73 mg	Cholesterol

Diabetic exchanges: Lean meat, ½;
very lean meat, 1; vegetable, 1; starch, 1

Garlic Toast with Cheese and Tomato

2   thick slices fat-free Italian bread
⅓   cup grated lowfat mozzarella cheese
1   clove garlic, pressed
½   teaspoon lemon juice
1   medium tomato, thinly sliced
2   teaspoons fat-free Italian salad dressing
½   teaspoon dried sweet basil

Spray small baking sheet or pan with nonstick cooking spray. Place slices of bread on baking sheet and place under the broiler until lightly browned. Turn bread over and brown on the other side.

In small bowl, combine cheese, garlic, and lemon juice, and toss and mix. Sprinkle this mixture evenly over toasted bread. Top with thin slices of tomato. Sprinkle each piece with Italian dressing and sprinkle with basil.

Place back under broiler for 1 to 2 minutes, or until cheese melts. This is wonderful with soups, salads, or pasta.

Each serving provides:

144	Calories	1.52	g	Fat
10.40 g	Protein	415	g	Sodium
22.88 g	Carbohydrate	3.93	mg	Cholesterol

Diabetic exchanges: Very lean meat, 1; vegetable, 1; starch, 1

Eggplant Sandwich on Focaccia Bread

SERVES 2

1 small eggplant, peeled and sliced
1 small onion, sliced
1 cup fresh mushrooms, sliced
1 strip of roasted sweet pepper, chopped
  Garlic salt to taste
  Black pepper to taste
2 slices of focaccia bread, 3½-inch square*
4 tablespoons shredded Parmesan cheese

*You can buy already prepared focaccia bread in bakeries and supermarkets, or you can make your own—depending on what best suits your time schedule.

Spray skillet with nonstick cooking spray. Add eggplant, onion, and mushrooms, and cook over medium-low heat, uncovered, for 6 to 8 minutes. Check for doneness. Cook a few minutes longer if eggplant is not done. Add roasted pepper, garlic salt, and black pepper. Simmer 1 or 2 minutes and remove from heat.

Slice the focaccia bread. Spread a generous portion of eggplant mixture on one side of the bread and add 2 tablespoons of shredded Parmesan cheese. Place top on sandwich. Repeat same for second sandwich. Enjoy.

Each serving provides:

296	Calories	6.85 g	Fat
14.56 g	Protein	578 g	Sodium
45.74 g	Carbohydrate	8.0 mg	Cholesterol

Diabetic exchanges: Lean meat, 2; vegetable, 1; starch, 2

Deluxe Garlic and Basil Bread

SERVES 10

4 cloves garlic, pressed
2 tablespoons hot water
1 tablespoon Molly McButter butter sprinkles
¼ cup white cooking wine
1 can of refrigerated pizza dough
½ cup fresh basil, chopped
1 cup fat-free shredded mozzarella cheese
  Garlic salt to taste
1 tablespoon fat-free liquid egg product
1 teaspoon sesame seeds

Preheat oven to 400 degrees.

Use small saucepan and combine garlic, hot water, Molly McButter, and cooking wine. Cook and stir over medium-low heat for 3 to 4 minutes. Remove from heat and allow to cool while preparing dough.

Remove pizza dough from canister and spread on clean dry surface. Add chopped fresh basil to cooled garlic mixture. Spread this mixture evenly over the surface of the dough. Sprinkle mozzarella cheese on surface. Add garlic salt to taste. Begin at one edge of the dough and roll. When roll is completely done, pinch edges together and place on baking sheet sprayed with nonstick cooking spray. Paint outside of roll with fat-free liquid egg product and sprinkle with sesame seeds.

Bake at 400 degrees for 20 to 25 minutes, or until outside of roll becomes a golden brown.

Each serving provides:

120	Calories	1.75 g	Fat
6.30 g	Protein	229 g	Sodium
18.09 g	Carbohydrate	2.0 mg	Cholesterol

Diabetic exchanges: Very lean meat, ½; starch, 1¼

Cheese and Mushroom Bread

Makes 12 Small Slices

2 cups fresh sliced mushrooms, browned and cooked
1 small onion, chopped
2 tablespoons finely chopped green pepper
1 roll of refrigerated pizza dough
1½ cups Kraft fat-free shredded mozzarella cheese
½ cup shredded Parmesan cheese
   Garlic salt to taste
   Black pepper to taste
2 tablespoons fat-free liquid egg product

Preheat oven to 350 degrees.

Spray skillet with nonstick cooking spray. Add mushrooms, onion, and green pepper. Stir and simmer over medium heat until lightly browned. Watch carefully, it burns easily.

Remove pizza dough from carton, spread on clean surface, and roll with rolling pin to enlarge dough. Retain the rectangular shape as you roll. Spread mushroom mixture over surface of dough. Add cheeses and sprinkle evenly over surface. Add garlic salt and black pepper if desired.

Starting at the edge of the dough, roll a couple of times, then fold each end inside toward the center. Continue rolling until completely rolled. Place on baking sheet sprayed with nonstick cooking spray. Pinch any creases in the dough and seal all edges. Paint top of loaf with fat-free liquid egg product using a pastry brush. Bake at 350 degrees for 30 minutes. Two slices equals 1 serving.

Each serving provides:

121	Calories	2.47 g	Fat
8.51 g	Protein	212 g	Sodium
16.12 g	Carbohydrate	5.17 mg	Cholesterol

Diabetic exchanges: Very lean meat, 1; starch, 1

Bread Circle with Garlic and Dill

  1 roll refrigerated pizza dough
  2 to 3 tablespoons skim milk
1½ cups Kraft fat-free mozzarella cheese
  1 teaspoon garlic salt
  ½ teaspoon dry dill weed
  1 tablespoon Molly McButter butter sprinkles
  2 tablespoons fat-free liquid egg product
  2 teaspoons sesame seeds

Preheat oven to 350 degrees.

Remove pizza dough from container and spread on clean dry surface. Use a rolling pin and roll out dough a little larger.

In small bowl, combine skim milk and shredded mozzarella cheese. Sprinkle cheese mixture evenly over dough surface. Sprinkle on garlic salt, dill weed, and Molly McButter.

Start on the long edge of dough and gently roll dough. After a couple of rolls, fold the ends toward the center, then continue rolling. Pinch all seams, or any place that cheese could leak out. Place on baking sheet sprayed with nonstick cooking spray and bend the ends of roll around to form a circle or horseshoe shape.

Paint outside of loaf with liquid egg product and then sprinkle on the sesame seeds. Bake in oven at 350 degrees for about 30 minutes. Remove and serve warm. Two slices equals 1 serving.

Each serving provides:

104	Calories	1.46 g	Fat
7.13 g	Protein	363 g	Sodium
15.07 g	Carbohydrate	2.54 mg	Cholesterol

Diabetic exchanges: Very lean meat, 1; starch, 1

Toasted Cheese Sandwich

SERVES 2

1   large onion, sliced and browned
1   hoagie bun (6-inch), lightly toasted
4   medium slices fresh tomato
½   cup Kraft fat-free mozzarella cheese
4   tablespoons fancy shredded Parmesan cheese
2   tablespoons fat-free Zesty Italian dressing
    Garlic salt to taste
    Black pepper to taste
1   teaspoon sesame seeds

Preheat broiler on Low.

Spray medium-sized skillet with nonstick cooking spray, add onion, and brown over medium to low heat. Stir often. Remove and set aside when onion is brown and tender.

Cut bun in half to make two separate halves. Spray with butter-flavored cooking spray and toast until golden brown.

Place buns on baking sheet or pan that has been sprayed with nonstick cooking spray. Arrange browned onion evenly on each bun, add 2 slices of tomato to each half. Add half the grated fat-free mozzarella cheese to each bun half. Add 2 tablespoons Parmesan cheese for each half. Sprinkle on Italian dressing, garlic salt, black pepper, and sesame seeds. Place under broiler just long enough to melt the cheese. Remove and serve hot.

Each serving provides:

344	Calories	5.63 g	Fat
21.0 g	Protein	998 g	Sodium
51.51 g	Carbohydrate	13.0 mg	Cholesterol

Diabetic exchanges: Lean meat, 3; vegetable, 1; starch, 2

Meatloaf Sandwich on Focaccia Bread

SERVES 2

¼ sweet bell pepper, sliced
1 small onion, sliced
   Salt and black pepper to taste
2 slices (½-inch) prepared garlic meatloaf
   (see page 144 for recipe)
2 pieces focaccia bread, 3½-inch square, sliced
4 tablespoons shredded Parmesan cheese

Spray skillet with nonstick cooking spray. Add bell peppers and onion and simmer and stir over low heat until vegetables are soft. Add salt and black pepper to taste. Place 1 slice of meatloaf on each piece of focaccia. Top with peppers and onion mixture and garnish each with 2 tablespoons shredded Parmesan cheese. Replace sandwich tops and serve.

Each serving provides:

248	Calories	9.10 g	Fat
14.49 g	Protein	555 g	Sodium
27.21 g	Carbohydrate	27.50 mg	Cholesterol

Diabetic exchanges: Lean meat, 2; vegetable, 2; starch, 1

Garlic Cheese Bread

1 hoagie-style sandwich bun
1 teaspoon Molly McButter butter sprinkles
½ cup Sargento lowfat mozzarella cheese
    Garlic salt to taste

Preheat oven to 400 degrees.

Slice sandwich bun in half, lengthwise. Spray each open face of bun with butter spray and sprinkle each half with ½ teaspoon Molly McButter. Spray baking pan or sheet with non-stick cooking spray. Place bun halves, sprayed side up, on the pan and place in oven at 400 degrees, until lightly browned.

    Remove from oven, add cheese to each half, and sprinkle on garlic salt to taste. Return to oven, just long enough to melt cheese. Serve warm.

Each serving provides:			
119	Calories	1.0 g	Fat
7.58 g	Protein	341 g	Sodium
19.45 g	Carbohydrate	2.50 mg	Cholesterol

Diabetic exchanges: Lean meat, ½; starch, 1½

INDEX

255

INTERNATIONAL CONVERSION CHART

These are not exact equivalents; they've been slightly rounded to make measuring easier.

LIQUID MEASUREMENTS

American	Imperial	Metric	Australian
2 tablespoons (1 oz.)	1 fl. oz.	30 ml	1 tablespoon
¼ cup (2 oz.)	2 fl. oz.	60 ml	2 tablespoons
⅓ cup (3 oz.)	3 fl. oz.	80 ml	¼ cup
½ cup (4 oz.)	4 fl. oz.	125 ml	⅓ cup
⅔ cup (5 oz.)	5 fl. oz.	165 ml	½ cup
¾ cup (6 oz.)	6 fl. oz.	185 ml	⅔ cup
1 cup (8 oz.)	8 fl. oz.	250 ml	¾ cup

SPOON MEASUREMENTS

American	Metric
¼ teaspoon	1 ml
½ teaspoon	2 ml
1 teaspoon	5 ml
1 tablespoon	15 ml

OVEN TEMPERATURES

Fahrenheit	Centigrade	Gas
250	120	½
300	150	2
325	160	3
350	180	4
375	190	5
400	200	6
450	230	8

WEIGHTS

US/UK	Metric
1 oz.	30 grams (g)
2 oz.	60 g
4 oz. (¼ lb)	125 g
5 oz. (⅓ lb)	155 g
6 oz.	185 g
7 oz.	220 g
8 oz. (½ lb)	250 g
10 oz.	315 g
12 oz. (¾ lb)	375 g
14 oz.	440 g
16 oz. (1 lb)	500 g
2 lbs.	1 kg

Finally, Food with Southwest Flair for Diabetics—and Their Families!

With this collection of more than 150 enticing soups, salads, side dishes, entrées, and desserts you will find it easy to maintain a diabetic diet without sacrificing flavor. Enjoy "real Mexican foods" such as:

- **Fiesta Tortilla Corn Chowder**
- **Chicken Taco Salad**
- **Cheesy Nachos**
- **Green Chili Quesadillas**
- **And many more!**

From the Author of *Real Food for People with Diabetes*

REAL Mexican FOOD
FOR PEOPLE WITH DIABETES

Dear Friends,

After being diagnosed with diabetes a few years ago, I decided to follow up my bestselling book *Fat Free and Ultra Lowfat Recipes* by writing a cookbook of tasty dishes for diabetics. There was such a terrific response from folks around the country to *Real Food for People with Diabetes* that I decided it was time we had our own cookbook of America's favorite ethnic food, Mexican and

(continued on back cover)

DORIS CROSS

ISBN 0-7615-1431-7 / Paperback / 288 pages
U.S. $15.00 / Can. $22.00

Prima HEALTH

To order, call (800) 632-8676 or visit us online at www.primahealth.com

At Last, Homestyle Foods for People with Diabetes— and Their Families!

You *can* limit the sugar and fat in your diet without skimping on flavor. The 150 easy and tempting "real food" recipes here will show you how. They include:

- **Chicken-Fried Chicken with Cream Gravy**
- **Cheesy Ham and Potato Chowder**
- **Ultra Lowfat Lasagna**
- **Chocolate Mousse Cheesecake**
- **And many more!**

Created by Doris Cross, these recipes will help you maintain a safe, healthful diet as a diabetic and continue to eat the meals you love.

From the Author of the Bestselling *Fat Free and Ultra Lowfat Recipes*

REAL FOOD
FOR PEOPLE WITH
DIABETES

DORIS CROSS with ALICE WILLIAMS

Dear Friends,
    As a recently diagnosed diabetic, I have struggled this past year to adapt to a new way of eating. I love food—all the old favorites and comfort foods. When I wrote my bestselling *Fat Free and Ultra Lowfat Recipes* I had just lost 100 pounds and needed to find
(Continued on back cover)

FOREWORD BY JANET POTTS, R.D.

ISBN 0-7615-1103-2 / Paperback / 272 pages
U.S. $15.00 / Can. $22.00

To order, call (800) 632-8676 or visit us online at www.primahealth.com

Also from Prima

Create Mouthwatering Recipes—Without the Fat!

Doris Cross' fat-free and ultra lowfat recipes have the satisfying taste you love! In this book, Doris combines recipes that are good for your health with the delicious, all-American taste you crave. Inside you'll find familiar dishes such as:

- **Green Chile Enchilada Casserole**
- **Hot & Spicy Chicken Salad**
- **Crispy Oven Potato Wedges**
- **Barbecue Burger Patties**
- **And more!**

ISBN 1-55958-584-6 / Comb bound / 240 pages
U.S. $14.95 / Can. $22.00

Prima
HEALTH

To order, call (800) 632-8676 or visit us online at www.primahealth.com

Now You Can Combat Diabetes and Hypoglycemia—Naturally!

Diabetes and hypoglycemia are two of the most common diseases and can lead to chronic metabolic problems. Often, traditional medications treat only specific symptoms without treating the whole body. Now, Dr. Michael Murray, one of the world's foremost authorities on nutrition and natural medicine, shows you how to take control of your blood sugar metabolism by using natural, healthful methods. Get expert naturopathic advice on:

- **Early symptoms and proper diagnosis**
- **Lifestyle choices and exercise**
- **Dietary guidelines, including 25 recipes**
- **And much, much more!**

Break the cycle of medication and begin a naturally healthful, balanced way of life!

ISBN 1-55958-426-2 / Paperback / 176 pages
U.S. $11.00 / Can. $16.00

**To order, call (800) 632-8676 or
visit us online at www.primahealth.com**

To Order Books

Please send me the following items:

Quantity	Title	Unit Price	Total
_____	Real Mexican Food for People with Diabetes	$ _15.00_	$ _____
_____	Real Food for People with Diabetes	$ _15.00_	$ _____
_____	Fat Free & Ultra Lowfat Recipes	$ _14.95_	$ _____
_____	Diabetes and Hypoglycemia	$ _11.00_	$ _____
_____	_____	$ _____	$ _____

Subtotal	$ _____
Deduct 10% when ordering 3-5 books	$ _____
7.25% Sales Tax (CA only)	$ _____
8.25% Sales Tax (TN only)	$ _____
5% Sales Tax (MD and IN only)	$ _____
7% G.S.T. Tax (Canada only)	$ _____
Shipping and Handling*	$ _____
Total Order	$ _____

*Shipping and Handling depend on Subtotal.

Subtotal	Shipping/Handling
$0.00–$14.99	$3.00
$15.00–$29.99	$4.00
$30.00–$49.99	$6.00
$50.00–$99.99	$10.00
$100.00–$199.99	$13.50
$200.00+	Call for Quote

**Foreign and all Priority Request orders:
Call Order Entry department
for price quote at 916-632-4400**
This chart represents the total retail price of books only (before applicable discounts are taken).

By Telephone: With American Express, MC or Visa, call 800-632-8676 or 916-632-4400. Mon–Fri, 8:30–4:30.

www.primapublishing.com

By E-mail: sales@primapub.com

By Mail: Just fill out the information below and send with your remittance to:

**Prima Publishing
P.O. Box 1260BK
Rocklin, CA 95677**

Name _____

Address _____

City _____ State _____ ZIP _____

MC/Visa/American Express# _____ Exp. _____

Check/money order enclosed for $ _____ Payable to Prima Publishing

Daytime telephone _____

Signature _____